SCIENTIFIC AMERICAN EXPLORES BIG IDEAS

Science and Gender

The Editors of *Scientific American*

SCIENTIFIC AMERICAN | EDUCATIONAL PUBLISHING

New York

Published in 2027 by Scientific American Educational Publishing
in association with **The Rosen Publishing Group**
2544 Clinton Street, Buffalo NY 14224

Contains material from Scientific American®, a division of Springer Nature America, Inc., reprinted by permission, as well as original material from The Rosen Publishing Group®.

First Edition

Scientific American
Lisa Pallatroni: Project Editor

Rosen Publishing
Nicole Horning: Compiling Editor
Michael Moy: Senior Graphic Designer

Cataloging-in-Publication Data
Names: Scientific American, Inc.
Title: Science and gender / edited by the Scientific American Editors.
Description: Buffalo, New York : Scientific American Educational Publishing, an imprint of Rosen Publishing, 2027. | Series: Scientific American explores big ideas | Includes glossary and index.
Identifiers: ISBN 9781538314586 (pbk.) | ISBN 9781538314593 (library bound) | ISBN 9781538314609 (ebook)
Subjects: LCSH: Gender expression–Juvenile literature. | Gender identity–Juvenile literature. | Gender-nonconforming people–Juvenile literature. | Gender-affirming care–Juvenile literature. | Transgender children–Juvenile literature.
Classification: LCC HQ18.552 S356 2027 | DDC 305.3–dc23

Manufactured in the United States of America
Websites listed were live at the time of publication.

Cover: Production Perig/Shutterstock.com

CPSIA Compliance Information: Batch # CS27SA.
For Further Information contact Rosen Publishing at 1-800-237-9932.

CONTENTS

INTRODUCTION

Gender is on a spectrum. It's about identity, expression, experiences, and the many ways society interacts with individuals who identify across the gender spectrum. Conversations about gender can be complex, emotional, and sometimes even difficult. But they are also essential for building awareness, respect, and safety for everyone.

This book is a collection of articles that explore different aspects of gender and the experiences of transgender and nonbinary individuals. In Gender-Affirming Care, you'll learn about the healthcare, resources, and approaches that support individuals in living authentically. Gender Expression examines how clothing, appearance, and behavior reflect personal identity and cultural influences. Gender and Sports looks at the unique challenges and opportunities transgender and nonbinary athletes face in competitive and recreational settings. Finally, Legislation and Violence explores how laws, policies, and social attitudes can both protect and threaten the safety and rights of gender-diverse communities.

Each chapter offers insight into the social, medical, and cultural dimensions of gender, emphasizing both challenges and progress to help you better understand the lived experiences of people navigating gender identity, while also learning how advocacy, education, and compassion can make a difference.

For some, navigating gender identity comes with additional challenges. Discrimination, bullying, legal obstacles, and violence can create stress, feelings of isolation, and depression. It's important to acknowledge that these pressures can impact mental health.

Editor's Note:
This book covers difficult topics like suicide, depression, and violence. Please take care of yourself and mental health while reading this book.

If you or someone you know are in crisis or thinking about suicide, support is available. Call or text **988**, *the Suicide & Crisis Lifeline, or use online chat at* **988lifeline.org**. *If you are elsewhere, local crisis hotlines or healthcare providers can connect you to help. You are not alone, and it's always okay to ask for support.*

Section 1: Gender-Affirming Care

What the Science on Gender-Affirming Care for Transgender Kids Really Shows

By Heather Boerner

Editor's Note (3/31/25): This article from 2022 describes attacks on gender-affirming care for transgender youth. Such attacks have increased in recent years, and many U.S. states have passed anti-trans legislation. President Donald Trump has also sought to limit such health care for transgender young people. Yet studies of gender-affirming care show it is generally safe, effective and often lifesaving.

For the first 40 years of their life, Texas resident Kelly Fleming spent a portion of most years in a deep depression. As an adult, Fleming–who uses they/them pronouns and who asked to use a pseudonym to protect their safety–would shave their face in the shower with the lights off so neither they nor their wife would have to confront the reality of their body.

What Fleming was experiencing, although they did not know it at the time, was gender dysphoria: the acute and chronic distress of living in a body that does not reflect one's gender and the desire to have bodily characteristics of that gender. While in therapy, Fleming discovered research linking access to gender-affirming hormone therapy with reduced depression in transgender people. They started a very low dose of estradiol, and the depression episodes became shorter, less frequent and less intense. Now they look at their body with joy.

So when Fleming sees what authorities in Texas, Alabama, Florida and other states are doing to bar transgender teens and children from receiving gender-affirming medical care, it infuriates them. And they are worried for their children, ages 12 and 14, both of whom are agender–a identity on the transgender spectrum that is neither masculine nor feminine.

"I'm just so excited to see them being able to present themselves in a way that makes them happy," Fleming says. "They are living their best life regardless of what others think, and that's a privilege that I did not get to have as a younger person."

Laws Based on "Completely Wrong" Information

Currently more than a dozen state legislatures or administrations are considering–or have already passed–laws banning health care for transgender young people. On April 20 the Florida Department of Health issued guidance to withhold such gender-affirming care. This includes social gender transitioning–acknowledging that a young person is trans, using their correct pronouns and name, and supporting their desire to live publicly as the gender of their experience rather than their sex assigned at birth. This comes nearly two months after Texas Governor Greg Abbott issued an order for the Texas Department of Family and Protective Services to investigate for child abuse parents who allow their transgender preteens and teenagers to receive medical care. Alabama recently passed SB 184, which would make it a felony to provide gender-affirming medical care to transgender minors. In Alabama, a "minor" is defined as anyone 19 or younger.

If such laws go ahead, 58,200 teens in the U.S. could lose access to or never receive gender-affirming care, according to the Williams Institute at the University of California, Los Angeles. A decade of research shows such treatment reduces depression, suicidality and other devastating consequences of trans preteens and teens being forced to undergo puberty in the sex they were assigned at birth).

The bills are based on "information that's completely wrong," says Michelle Forcier, a pediatrician and professor of pediatrics at Brown University. Forcier literally helped write the book on how to provide evidence-based gender care to young people. She is also an assistant dean of admissions at the Warren Alpert Medical School of Brown University. Those laws "are absolutely, absolutely incorrect" about the science of gender-affirming care for young people, she says. "[Inaccurate information] is there to create drama. It's there to make people take a side."

The truth is that data from more than a dozen studies of more than 30,000 transgender and gender-diverse young people consistently show that access to gender-affirming care is associated with better mental health outcomes–and that lack of access to such care is associated with higher rates of suicidality, depression and self-harming behavior. (Gender diversity refers to the extent to which a person's gendered behaviors, appearance and identities are culturally incongruent with the sex they were assigned at birth. Gender-diverse people can identify along the transgender spectrum, but not all do.) Major medical organizations, including the American Academy of Pediatrics (AAP), the American Academy of Child and Adolescent Psychiatry, the Endocrine Society, the American Medical Association, the American Psychological Association and the American Psychiatric Association, have published policy statements and guidelines on how to provide age-appropriate gender-affirming care. All of those medical societies find such care to be evidence-based and medically necessary.

AAP and Endocrine Society guidelines call for developmentally appropriate care, and that means no puberty blockers or hormones until young people are already undergoing puberty for their sex assigned at birth. For one thing, "there are no hormonal differences among prepubertal children," says Joshua Safer, executive director of the Mount Sinai Center for Transgender Medicine and Surgery in New York City and co-author of the Endocrine Society's guidelines. Those guidelines provide the option of gonadotropin-releasing hormone analogues (GnRHas), which block the release of sex hormones, once young people are already into the second of five puberty stages–marked by breast budding and pubic hair. These are offered only if a teen is not ready to make decisions about puberty. Access to gender-affirming hormones and potential access to gender-affirming surgery is available at age 16–and then, in the case of transmasculine youth, only mastectomy, also known as top surgery. The Endocrine Society does not recommend genital surgery for minors.

Before puberty, gender-affirming care is about supporting the process of gender development rather than directing children through a specific course of gender transition or maintenance of cisgender presentation, says Jason Rafferty, co-author of AAP's policy statement on gender-affirming care and a pediatrician and psychiatrist at Hasbro Children's Hospital in Rhode Island. "The current research suggests that, rather than predicting or preventing who a child might become, it's better to value them for who they are now–even at a young age," Rafferty says.

A Safe Environment to Explore Gender

A 2021 systematic review of 44 peer-reviewed studies found that parent connectedness, measured by a six-question scale asking about such things as how safe young people feel confiding in their guardians or how cared for they feel in the family, is associated with greater resilience among teens and young adults who are transgender or gender-diverse. Rafferty says he sees his role with regard to prepubertal children as offering a safe environment for the child to explore their gender and for parents to ask questions. "The gender-affirming approach is not some railroad of people to hormones and surgery," Safer says. "It is talking and watching and being conservative."

Only once children are older, and if the incongruence between the sex assigned to them at birth and their experienced gender has persisted, does discussion of medical transition occur. First a gender therapist has to diagnose the young person with gender dysphoria.

After a gender dysphoria diagnosis–and only if earlier conversations suggest that hormones are indicated–guidelines call for discussion of fertility, puberty suppression and hormones. Puberty-suppressing medications have been used for decades for cisgender children who start puberty early, but they are not meant to be used indefinitely. The Endocrine Society guidelines recommend a maximum of two years on GnRHa therapy to allow more time for children to form their gender identity before undergoing puberty for their sex assigned at birth, the effects of which are irreversible.

"[Puberty blockers] are part of the process of 'do no harm,'" Forcier says, referencing a popular phrase that describes the Hippocratic Oath, which many physicians recite a version of before they begin to practice.

Hormone blocker treatment may have side effects. A 2015 longitudinal observational cohort study of 34 transgender young people found that, by the time the participants were 22 years old, trans women experienced a decrease in bone mineral density. A 2020 study of puberty suppression in gender-diverse and transgender young people found that those who started puberty blockers in early puberty had lower bone mineral density *before* the start of treatment than the public at large. This suggests, the authors wrote, that GnRHa use may not be the cause of low bone mineral density for these young people. Instead they found that lack of exercise was a primary factor in low bone-mineral density, especially among transgender girls.

Other side effects of GnRHa therapy include weight gain, hot flashes and mood swings. But studies have found that these side effects—and puberty delay itself—are reversible, Safer says.

Gender-affirming hormone therapy often involves taking an androgen blocker (a chemical that blocks the release of testosterone and other androgenic hormones) and estrogen in transfeminine teens, and testosterone supplementation in transmasculine teens. Such hormones may be associated with some physiological changes for adult transgender people. For instance, transfeminine people taking estrogen see their so-called "good" cholesterol increase. By contrast, transmasculine people taking testosterone see their good cholesterol decrease. Some studies have hinted at effects on bone mineral density, but these are complicated and also depend on personal, family history, exercise, and many other factors in addition to hormones."

And while some critics point to decade-old study and older studies suggesting very few young people persist in transgender identity into late adolescence and adulthood, Forcier says the data are "misleading and not accurate." A recent review detailed methodological problems with some of these studies. New research in 17,151 people who had ever socially transitioned found that 86.9 percent persisted in their gender identity. Of the 2,242 people who reported that they reverted to living as the gender associated with the sex they were assigned at birth, just 15.9 percent said they did so because of internal factors such as questioning their experienced gender but also because of fear, mental health issues and suicide attempts. The rest reported the cause was social, economic and familial stigma and discrimination. A third reported that they ceased living openly as a trans person because doing so was "just too hard for me."

The Harms of Denying Care

Data suggest the effects of denying that care are worse than whatever side effects result from delaying sex-assigned-at-birth puberty. And medical society guidelines conclude that the benefits of gender-affirming care outweigh the risks. Without gender-affirming hormone therapy, cisgender hormones take over, forcing body changes that can be permanent and distressing.

A 2020 study of 300 gender-incongruent young people found that mental distress—including self-harm, suicidal thoughts and depression—increased as the children were made to proceed with puberty according to their assigned sex. By the time 184 older teens (with a median age of 16) reached the stage in which transgender boys began their periods and grew breasts and transgender girls' voice dropped and facial hair began to appear, 46 percent had been diagnosed with depression, 40 percent had self-harmed, 52 percent had considered suicide, and 17 percent had attempted it—rates significantly higher than those of gender-incongruent children who were a median of 13.9 years old or of cisgender kids their own age.

Conversely, access to gender-affirming hormones in adolescence appears to have a protective effect. In one study, researchers followed 104 teens and young adults for a year and asked them about their depression, anxiety and suicidality at the time they started receiving hormones or puberty blockers and again at the three-month, six-month and one-year mark. At the beginning of the study, which was published in *JAMA Network Open* in February 2022, more than half of the respondents reported moderate to severe depression, half reported moderate to severe anxiety, and 43.3 percent reported thoughts of self-harm or suicide in the past two weeks.

But when the researchers analyzed the results based on the kind of gender-affirming care the teens had received, they found that those who had access to puberty blockers or gender-affirming hormones were 60 percent less likely to experience moderate to severe depression. And those with access to the medical treatments were 73 percent less likely to contemplate self-harm or suicide.

"Delays in prescribing puberty blockers and hormones may in fact worsen mental health symptoms for trans youth," says Diana Tordoff, an epidemiology graduate student at the University of Washington and co-author of the study.

That effect may be lifelong. A 2022 study of more than 21,000 transgender adults showed that just 41 percent of adults who wanted hormone therapy received it, and just 2.3 percent had access to it in adolescence. When researchers looked at rates of suicidal thinking over the past year in these same adults, they found that access to hormone therapy in early adolescence was associated with a 60 percent reduction in suicidality in the past year and that access in late adolescence was associated with a 50 percent reduction.

For Fleming's kids in Texas, gender-affirming hormones are not currently part of the discussion; not all trans people desire hormones or surgery to feel affirmed in their gender. But Fleming is already looking at jobs in other states to protect their children's access to such care, should they change their mind. "Getting your body closer to the gender [you] identify with–that is what helps the dysphoria," Fleming says. "And not giving people the opportunity to do that, making it harder for them to do that, is what has made the suicide rate among transgender people so high. We just–trans people are just trying to survive."

About the Author

Heather Boerner is a health care and science journalist based in Pittsburgh. Her work has appeared in the Daily Beast, *the* Washington Post, *the* Atlantic, *and NPR. Follow her on Twitter @HeatherBoerner*

Transgender Youth Have Better Emotional Health after Taking Hormones, New Study Finds

By Tyler Santora

Suicide attempts among transgender and nonbinary youth jumped by as much as 72 percent from 2018 to 2022 in states that had recently passed laws to curtail their rights. And President Donald Trump took this onslaught to the federal level last month when he signed an executive order to cut federal medical care support for trans people aged 19 and younger, which two federal judges have since temporarily blocked. These political actions affect a set of young people who already had much higher rates of depression, anxiety, self-harm and suicide attempts than their nontransgender peers. Many of the recent state laws ban gender-affirming care–which a 2022 study suggests is a lifeline for many trans youth. In the study, those who received gender-affirming care had 60 percent lower odds of depression and 73 percent lower odds of suicidality over a 12-month follow-up than those who did not.

A growing body of evidence supports the mental health benefits of gender-affirming care for trans youth–including puberty blockers, hormone therapy and, in very rare cases, surgery. Now a new study adds to this evidence: it's the first of its kind to show that hormone therapy improves overall emotional health among trans youth.

For the new study, published in January in the *Journal of Adolescent Health*, researchers tracked the emotional health of 315 trans youth aged 12 to 20 for two years after they began using hormone therapy (testosterone or estrogen). Emotional health is a component of mental health that concerns feelings; it shapes how we act in relationships, react to struggles and generally behave in everyday life. The study also tracked appearance congruence, a measure of how much a person's physical presentation matches their gender identity.

Over two years, appearance congruence (based on a validated nine-question metric) improved in tandem with all five domains of emotional health: psychological well-being; self-efficacy, or the belief that one can achieve one's goals; social satisfaction, including friendship, emotional support and loneliness; negative social perception, or perceived hostility and rejection; and negative affect, or anger, sadness and fear.

Before taking hormones, the participants, on average, had what the authors called "clinically concerning" scores in the areas of friendship and life satisfaction. After just six months of taking hormones, however, these averages reached healthy levels. The study authors declined to comment on the findings.

"This adds to a body of literature that's already shown improvements in mental health outcomes and safety," says Jae Corman, an affiliate assistant professor of health systems management and policy at Oregon Health & Science University and head of analytics and research at gender-affirming care service FOLX Health. "This is another important dimension: emotional health." Corman was not involved in the new study.

Emotional health often doesn't receive as much public attention as the broader category of mental health, but the study authors write that it's crucial to the latter–and to physical health as well. Higher psychological well-being and perceived social support, for example, are associated with lower rates of disease and death. Positive mood is linked to school engagement, sleep quality and increased exercise, and negative mood is associated with a weakened immune system. Loneliness in young people is correlated with depression and anxiety symptoms, problematic alcohol use and an increased risk of long-term mental illness.

Trans youth who hadn't undergone significant puberty-related changes before starting hormones–either because they took puberty blockers or had late-onset puberty–had better psychological well-being and negative affect scores before starting hormones than those who had already begun puberty. The study authors write that this may be because those who are able to access puberty blockers are more likely to have supportive families with the ability to afford the medication. Or, they add, it could be because they hadn't yet developed unwanted secondary sex characteristics such as breasts or facial hair.

Despite studies indicating the benefits of gender-affirming care for trans youth, 23 states have bans in effect, and two additional states have banned surgeries. Trump's recent executive order takes things further: it could withdraw federal funding from hospitals that provide it and drop it from Medicaid coverage.

Trump's new executive order calls the evidence supporting gender-affirming care for trans youth "junk science." But numerous medical organizations, including the American Academy of Pediatrics and the American Medical Association, support transition-related care for youth, citing decades of research. "This research, as well as the clinical experience of [experts] who specialize in treating gender dysphoria show that the use of these medications to treat adolescents is both safe and effective in appropriately identified individuals," medical organizations, including the American Academy of Pediatrics, wrote in an amicus brief to the Supreme Court for a case that will decide whether states can ban gender-affirming care for trans youth.

"What we keep seeing is positive results published in top-tier journals," Corman says. "These are really scrutinized papers and heavily peer-reviewed, so I think we can trust the evidence here."

"You get end results where kids are happier, less likely to engage in self-harm and more likely to be resilient and adaptive," says Ralph Vetters, medical director at the Sidney Borum Jr. Health Program, a health center for LGBTQ+ and disadvantaged young people. "That's what you want for any child, [transgender] or [cisgender]."

Gender-affirming hormones are generally safe for adolescents, Vetters adds. When such hormones do raise the risk of a condition, that increase is typically to the risk level associated with a given sex, he says. When people assigned male at birth take estrogen through a skin patch, for example, their blood clot risk increases from the typical male level to the typical female one.

The safety of gender-affirming hormone therapy for trans youth is backed up by the fact that, for decades, these hormones have been prescribed to cisgender youth with hypogonadism, a condition in which the gonads don't properly release sex hormones. "Negative things are not happening to these youth," Vetters says.

A common argument against gender-affirming care is that it's offered too readily to young people, including those who haven't reached a developmental stage appropriate for certain types of care, and that they might later regret transitioning. But a recent four-year study led by Corman suggested that gender-affirming hormone use is rare among adolescents and that it isn't being prescribed to anyone younger than age 12. Another recent study found that only 0.5 percent of trans adolescents who start hormones later stop because they reidentify with the gender they were assigned at birth.

Another hesitation with hormones is that they may impair future fertility. Vetters says recent research suggests that testosterone may not permanently impair fertility, and at least some transgender men have been to get pregnant after stopping hormone therapy, though the effects are still unclear. The extent to which estrogen impairs sperm production, and to which its effects are reversible, isn't as well researched, though Vetters says it does have some permanent effects. There are, however, options for fertility preservation, including sperm and egg cryopreservation (for those who have already undergone puberty) or testicular and ovarian tissue cryopreservation.

The bottom line, Corman says, is that gender-affirming hormone treatment is working: "It's being prescribed as clinically necessary. So there's really no need to ban this type of care."

About the Author

Tyler Santora is a Colorado-based science journalist and the health and science editor at Fatherly.

Transgender Kids: What Does It Take to Help Them Thrive?

By Francine Russo

Skyler was counting down the days. In just a few months, the 14-year-old would attend a life-changing medical appointment. It would be the first step toward resolving body and identity issues that the teenager had been struggling with for years.

Skyler's sex at birth (or, to use trans terminology, his "assigned" gender) was female, yet he did not readily identify as a girl. From the age of four, Skyler hated wearing dresses, which he would rip apart with scissors. "It didn't feel like me," he says. Later he did not understand why he was told not to play football, soccer and kickball with the boys.

His confusion grew painful over time. Skyler's first period, at age 11, was traumatic. Every month he would spend an entire week at home, unable to face school. "I was at war with myself," he says, "and I struggled with depression. I'd pick at my skin and cut myself on my arms and shoulders and legs to distract myself."

By seventh grade he had learned about transgender identities at his public school. There had been a few other transgender children in the district, and he realized he felt trans. He began binding his size-DD breasts, albeit awkwardly and painfully, and investigating blogs, articles and YouTube videos on being transgender. He learned about puberty blockers, which could stop all further sexual development, but given how womanly his body had already become, thought–mistakenly–it might be too late for that option. "I just started to give up," he says. "And that's about the time I came out to my mom."

His mother, Corina, a preschool teacher, had long been concerned about Skyler's gender issues. She was supportive and, with the help of transgender advocate Aidan Key of Gender Odyssey, began seeking experts to help her child. In eighth grade Skyler came out at school, becoming the first openly trans kid there. Although there was some fumbling at first, the teachers began adopting masculine pronouns for him and using his new trans name, Skyler. After a long struggle with the administrators, the school finally created one gender-neutral bathroom for him to use.

Despite these initial hurdles at school, the cutting stopped. He finally felt "more at peace" with himself. But the challenge of a medically assisted biological transition remained. After a long wait, Skyler at last had an appointment set for November. The doctor would examine his physical health and review his gender history, psychological health, emotional maturity and a host of other details. But what would follow was unclear. In a case like this, a physician might prescribe puberty blockers to stall further development or—as Skyler hoped—cross-sex hormones to begin the development of more masculine attributes. As the days ticked down, his excitement grew: "It's so hard to wait until November. I go to sleep and wake up, and I think, 'Is today November?' But it isn't, and I have to wait, and it's so long!"

It is hard to imagine a more momentous and complex set of decisions than those faced by young trans people like Skyler and the clinicians who seek to help them. As the media has spotlighted trans celebrities such as television personality Caitlyn Jenner and actress Laverne Cox and as society begins to better understand and accept trans people (perhaps even in the U.S. military), demand for medical and psychological support has exploded. But the biggest challenge—medically, psychologically and ethically—is the growing number of children (some as young as seven or eight) seeking treatment despite uncertain medical science. Distressed but supportive parents have been flooding the small number of U.S. clinics that specialize in helping transgender youth. In Los Angeles, for example, the Center for Transyouth Health and Development saw close to 400 patients in 2014 versus 40 in 2008. The center is currently adding three to four new patients a week.

No one can say how many transgender people are out there. A 2011 meta-analysis of population surveys from the University of California, Los Angeles's Williams Institute suggests that 0.3 percent of people in the U.S. feel strongly that they are transgender. One of the studies included in the analysis–from the University of Michigan–found that between 0.1 and 0.5 percent of Americans have taken medical steps to transition. Whether these individuals take those steps or not, they are a vulnerable population. Transgender youth, according to a 2015 Boston-based study of data from electronic health records, face two to three times the risk of their peers for serious psychological issues, such as depression, anxiety disorders, self-harm and suicide. They urgently require attention.

Yet this area of medicine is so new that few clinics have enough qualified and experienced professionals to adequately screen these children and youth. A protocol, developed by Dutch scientists in the early 2000s and adopted by the international Endocrine Society, serves as a guideline for doctors helping young people transition, and researchers have recently confirmed that this approach yields good results for most patients. But clinicians are now debating how closely to follow it. A growing number of trans experts believe the recommendations are too cautious, that screening procedures are too onerous and that young people are forced to wait too long for treatment that could alleviate their misery. Veterans in the field counter that caution is essential given that treatment is largely irreversible and that gender identity can be fluid in the young, with some patients having second thoughts. A paucity of research makes it difficult for both sides to resolve the debate and determine what is best for their patients.

Insistent, Consistent and Persistent

As newly alerted parents arrive at clinics with boys who sew and dress in frilly outfits and girls who would not be caught dead doing either, experts have to diagnose whether these children have gender dysphoria. In this condition, people suffer distress because of a mismatch between the gender identity they experience and their biological sex as determined by chromosomes, gonads and genitals.

(Until 2012, psychiatrists classified the condition as "gender identity disorder," a term now viewed as stigmatizing.)

Although adolescents may confuse the two, gender identity is different from sexual orientation. Norman P. Spack, a pediatrician, pediatric endocrinologist and founder of the gender clinic at Boston Children's Hospital, borrows language from one of his first transgender patients to explain: "Sexual orientation is who you go to bed with. Gender identity is who you go to bed as." In fact, Spack adds, "I could never predict the sexual orientation of my patients."

Furthermore, gender dysphoria is more than just rejecting the social and cultural roles assigned to a given gender. Many kids push back against these norms–as when a young boy rejects macho roughhousing to playing house or a girl prefers toy soldiers to dolls–without any discomfort regarding sexual or gender identity.

But for some children, there is a nagging, painful conviction that the gender they are forced to present to the world does not reflect their true self. "There's a small subgroup of trans kids who, as soon as they can talk, are saying, 'I'm not the gender you think I am,'" says psychologist Diane Ehrensaft of the Child and Adolescent Gender Center at the University of California, San Francisco, Benioff Children's Hospital. Often, Ehrensaft says, these kids do not like their bodies.

Among children under the age of about 12 who cross-identify, in terms of how they dress and behave, only a minority will continue to see themselves as transgender after puberty. A 2008 study by psychologists Madeleine S. C. Wallien and Peggy T. Cohen-Kettenis, both then at VU University Medical Center in Amsterdam, followed 77 children who had been diagnosed with gender dysphoria between the ages of five and 12. At age 16 or later the researchers found that 43 percent of the teens were no longer gender-dysphoric and that 27 percent remained so (some could not be reached for follow-up). Of those who stopped cross-identifying, all the girls and half of the boys were heterosexual; the other half of the boys were either homosexual or bisexual.

In what has become the mantra of the field for recognizing clear-cut trans children, they are "insistent, consistent and persistent over time" in their identification with the gender opposite to the one that they were assigned. A 2013 study led by Thomas D. Steensma, a psychologist at VU University Medical Center, confirmed that the intensity and persistence of identifying with the opposite, nonassigned gender are powerful indicators in predicting who will remain trans. Working with 79 boys and 48 girls referred for gender dysphoria to VU University Medical Center before age 12, Steensma and his colleagues measured these factors through a questionnaire assessing cross-gender behavior through early childhood. At age 15 or later only 23 of the boys and 24 of the girls had persisted. Those who remained trans were more likely to have been insistent early on, saying, for example, "I am a boy" rather than "I wish I were a boy" or they would grow up to be a daddy, not a mommy. Still, Steensma cautions, it is hard to predict whether any specific child will persist as transgender.

Some children change their mind at critical junctures, such as after undergoing a "social transition" (changing their name, pronoun and appearance to live in their affirmed gender) or taking puberty blockers. Some children, Ehrensaft says, gradually realize that they are trans. Still others are more focused on gender expression: wishing to be the other gender and cross-dressing but in a playful, fantasy context, without any distress about their body. Some, she says, are "proto-gay" and likely in adolescence to come out as gay, lesbian or bisexual. Increasingly, many will identify as gender queer, saying, in effect, "I do not identify with either gender; I'm beyond gender" or "I do not fit into your male/female binary." Such kids, Ehrensaft says, "are our littlest gender outlaws."

Teens who identify as trans, says psychologist Laura Edwards-Leeper of Pacific University, may also be reacting to peer influences, family dynamics, or religious or cultural beliefs. In some cultures, for example, she says, individuals face less stigma for being transgender than for being homosexual. So it is complicated.

Setting the Standard

In many respects, the Netherlands serves as an exemplar for supporting trans and gender-questioning people. In October, Loiza Lamers won Holland's Next Top Model, the first transgender winner from any country. One Dutch teenager (who appears on our cover at age 10) began her social transition early in life and feels that her experiences today are no different than those of her contemporaries. "I'm like any other high school girl," she says. "I love my dogs, spending lots of time with my girlfriends, going dancing."

The degree of social acceptance in the Netherlands may reflect the country's long history working with the trans community. Since 1975 clinicians at VU University Medical Center have counseled 5,000 adults and helped many hundreds of people transition to a different gender. As younger people came forward seeking guidance, Dutch experts established a second clinic for children and adolescents at University Medical Center Utrecht in 1987 that has since joined VU University Medical Center's clinic, known as the Center of Expertise on Gender Dysphoria. To date, they have counseled 1,000 young people, including some who, like the Dutch teen, have pursued a transition.

The procedure these clinicians developed became a template of sorts for the *Endocrine Society's guidelines and the World Professional Association for Transgender Health's Standards of Care*, now used around the world. The protocol first requires a series of psychological assessments. Given the potential fluidity of identity in a young person, careful screening is considered essential to identify which children should undertake the process of transitioning. Assuming kids meet the diagnosis of gender dysphoria, clinicians advise parents to wait until after puberty to see whether their child will persist. (Meanwhile many parents, with or without clinicians' encouragement, may help their children make a social transition before puberty.) At what doctors refer to as Tanner stage 2, when girls have tiny breast buds and boys have slightly enlarged testes, they can receive puberty blockers to prevent further sexual maturation.

This stage's onset is variable but usually occurs between 10 and 12 years of age. At around age 16 those who persistently identify as transgender can receive cross-sex hormones, and at 18 they can elect to have gender-reassignment surgery. Throughout the process, the transitioning person must receive mental health support.

According to the first long-term research findings, young people who receive this kind of care do quite well. A 2014 study by psychiatrist Annelou L. C. de Vries of VU University Medical Center and her colleagues reported good results for 55 young people followed from before puberty suppression until after cross-sex hormonal treatment and surgery. Over this period, their psychological functioning steadily improved–with declining levels of gender dysphoria and anxiety and a greater sense of overall happiness. After treatment, their sense of well-being was similar to that of their peers who were not trans. All these transgender youth had identified as trans in childhood, de Vries says.

These recent positive outcomes are based on strict adherence to the protocols. But increasingly in both the U.S. and the Netherlands, with this research as a baseline, clinicians are making treatment decisions on a case-by-case basis. Guidelines recommend waiting until 18 for body-altering surgery, for instance, but some trans boys are having the most common operation–"top surgery," or breast removal–as early as 13 because binding breasts can cause pain or physical problems.

Even the Endocrine Society is revising its guidelines to be more flexible, says society committee member Stephen Rosenthal, a pediatric endocrinologist at the U.C.S.F. School of Medicine. Although "around 16" will still be the recommended age for cross-sex hormones, for example, newer standards will recognize "compelling reasons" to start earlier, such as to safeguard a child's physical or emotional welfare.

Parents are part of the push to address cases more individually. Gender transitions are complex at any age, but for a minor there is the added complication of reliance on adult guardians for consent and support.

Helping Younger Children Thrive

At age three Marlo Mack reports, her child looked in her eyes and said, "Mama, something went wrong when I was in your tummy that made me come out as a boy instead of a girl. Put me back so I can come out again as a girl." For nearly a year Mack resisted her child's entreaties to be a girl. Then she grieved for her lost little boy and loved and accepted her new daughter, a "girl with a penis."

Their therapist, Mack says, urged her to "take a wait-and-see attitude," at least until age five, before supporting a social transition. "I tried to do it," Mack says, "but I felt unsupportive and almost abusive." Thus, at the age of four and a half, Mack's child became a girl at home and in the world.

There is no medical treatment for prepubescent transgender children, but a growing community of clinicians is cautiously endorsing social transitions. Mack is one of an increasing number of parents in the U.S. who are helping their preschoolers to live as the gender they feel they are. In the Netherlands before the year 2000, Steensma says, almost none of the children referred to the Amsterdam clinic for gender dysphoria were presenting socially as their affirmed gender. By 2009 that percentage had risen to more than 33 percent, a reflection of similar parental support.

The most important question surrounding a social transition, according to psychiatrist Scott Leibowitz of Ann & Robert H. Lurie Children's Hospital of Chicago, is whether it helps the child thrive. Suppose a boy will not go to school except in a dress? "If a kid does go to school in a dress and does well," Leibowitz says, "I support it."

There is one big caveat for parents: be open to your child changing back. Families who, for example, have grieved their lost daughter and finally, painfully, accepted their new son may find it difficult to tolerate the ambiguity of their loss/gain. With the greatest love and best of intentions, they can trap their child in a mold that no longer fits. Edwards-Leeper recalls one patient who told her, "I can't change my mind. My parents have done so much for me."

In a 2011 review of adolescents at the Amsterdam clinic, Steensma found that children who had transitioned socially were indeed more likely to remain trans than those who had not come out in their community. But he is unsure whether the social transition helped or hindered all of these kids. For instance, Steensma says, two adolescent girls who were no longer trans struggled for some time to change back to their female identity because of "fear of teasing and shame to admit they had been wrong." He wonders whether counseling children on coping with their gender variance until early puberty might be a lesser evil than having them make a complete social transition twice, including a name and pronoun change.

"One True Test of Gender"

Adolescence is a powerful time—physically, psychologically and socially—in determining lasting gender identity, experts say. At this point, young people often decide who they are and are not. Some young people may discover they are or may be trans. In a 2011 qualitative study of 25 teens, Steensma found that along with feelings about the changes in their bodies, the children's responses to a new social environment provided clues to their gender identity. They were now confronting a world in which boys and girls divide and hang out with their same-sex peers. They might have also been experiencing their first sexual and romantic feelings.

Despite pressure from an increasing number of parents to use blockers before Tanner stage 2 and the onset of puberty, the medical community agrees that waiting is essential. "Some parents are so convinced their child is trans," Spack says, "that they don't want their child to have any natural hormones. These parents bring their kids in as young as age seven or eight. If we did that, we'd take away the one true test of gender: puberty. If the kid accepts the body they get at puberty, how can the parents say, 'My child is in the wrong body?'"

At or after Tanner stage 2, endocrinologists administer puberty suppression through either leuprolide acetate injections on a regular basis or surgical insertion of an implant that slowly releases histrelin. These are drugs that mimic the body's natural signal to stop producing hormones.

Doctors who treat trans kids say that puberty blockers are probably safe. Initially there had been concern about a negative impact on bone density, which normally increases during puberty. Fortunately, studies that followed children who had taken these drugs for "precocious puberty" into adulthood found that they appeared to have relatively normal bone density and no other serious effects–at least for the 30-year follow-up period, says pediatric endocrinologist Daniel Metzger of BC Children's Hospital in Vancouver.

After kids stop taking blockers, the effects disappear within six months, and they resume their natal puberty or take cross-sex hormones and go through puberty as their affirmed gender. Some kids remain on blockers when they take cross-hormones to prevent any unwanted pubertal changes that could happen on small doses of cross-hormones.

The medical purpose is to temporarily halt menstruation and the development of breasts, beards and other sexual characteristics, reducing the need for later surgeries and procedures and enhancing the quality of any gender change. Doctors often determine the length of treatment to prolong growth for trans boys and to curtail height for trans girls.

Psychologically, blockers reduce the distress of adolescents who, like Skyler, might otherwise harm themselves in reaction to pubertal changes. Most of all, puberty suppression gives young adolescents additional time to mature, to determine their true gender identity and to more fully evaluate the irreversible effects of taking the next step: cross-sex hormones.

Despite compelling need, some adolescents cannot get blockers. They may be too far into puberty when they recognize themselves as trans or may not be able to afford the treatment, which is often not covered by insurance. Injections of leuprolide acetate cost $700 to $1,500 a month, and histrelin implant surgery totals about $15,000. Cheaper substitutes such as progesterone have potentially serious side effects, including the risk of blood clots. For these reasons, some doctors may start young teens on more affordable cross-sex hormones instead of blockers.

A Rift in the Field

At each stage of transitioning, parents and clinicians have begun questioning the existing standards, particularly for children who appear to be "clearly" trans and therefore might benefit from a different approach. Some of these transgender youth specialists, such as pediatrician Johanna Olson, director of the Center for Transyouth Health and Development at Children's Hospital Los Angeles, consider themselves as advocates for the children. "We have no specific, lengthy, neuropsychiatric screening protocol," Olson says of her clinic. She feels that current measures of gender dysphoria are inadequate. "Our model is to listen to the young people. They are like snowflakes. They each need an approach that is individually tailored to their needs."

Perhaps the most controversial issue in the transitioning process is how long teens should wait before taking cross-sex hormones–for trans females, this means estrogen and antiandrogens; for trans males, testosterone. Among their other results, estrogens produce feminizing effects such as enlarging breasts and distributing fat in a more female pattern. Testosterone halts menstruation, promotes the growth of masculine-type body hair, male muscle mass, voice deepening and other male characteristics.

Depending on when puberty begins, it could easily take half a decade before someone qualifies for this step, according to the strict protocol. More and more, the "advocate" side of the field has called to stop keeping these children "on the sidelines" while their peers go through puberty. For clear-cut trans kids, therefore, many clinicians are increasingly comfortable giving cross-sex hormones at 14 or even younger.

But veteran practitioners, such as Edwards-Leeper, worry about moving too fast. As at other stages, the concern remains that a young person may not persist in a trans identity yet feel pressured to continue. Some patients, she says, feel as though they are "'stuck' in a gender or on a runaway train that is hard to get off." And unlike earlier stages, the stakes are higher: cross-sex hormones have irreversible effects on physical development.

Added complications arise with adolescents who only at puberty discover they may be trans. Payton McPhee of British Columbia is an example. A tomboy as a child, Payton began questioning his gender at 11 as friends began getting crushes. At 13 he realized he was attracted to girls. He came out as a lesbian, he says, "but it still didn't feel right." At 14 he met his first trans person and looked up "female-to-male" online. He was transfixed. "I was excited to finally have something to call myself," he says.

With the support of his parents and doctors, Payton began taking birth-control pills to reduce his period to twice a year. By binding his breasts and doing vocal exercises to lower his voice, he says, he can "pass" as a boy. Now 15, he would like testosterone therapy. But his parents and doctors are not yet convinced. "His psychiatrist said that at the very least, Payton is gender-fluid," reports his mother, Sarah McPhee, "and most likely transgender."

Clinicians are seeing kids like Payton show up in increasing numbers. But whether they should get cross-sex hormones, wait or take small doses for a short time to "explore" their gender is an open question. Some kids may be confused, says Harvard Medical School psychologist and gender expert Amy Tishelman, "and this is a way to glom onto an identity." These kids may turn out to be trans. Or they may be more gender-fluid and need to experiment.

Dianne Berg, a psychologist and gender expert at the University of Minnesota, has seen some transitioning adolescents who identify as neither stereotypically male nor female and have parents pushing them to fit a more traditional mold. "It is hard for parents to wrap their head around their teen saying, 'I want to be a man, but I don't want to be a manly man–I want to be a more feminine kind of man,'" Berg says.

Metzger recalls a female-to-male patient who, at 13, wanted to transition and, at 16, got testosterone. Halfway through treatment, when the patient had a little facial hair and a bit more male bone structure, he asked to go on a lower dose, telling his doctor he was "a femme kind of boy." Metzger believes he has since had his ovaries removed and has remained on a lower dose of testosterone. "Is that *safe?*" the endocrinologist asks. "No one knows the answers."

Difficult Trade-Offs

One of the thorniest issues about age is whether an 11- or even 14-year-old can understand the implications of a treatment that means he or she can never have biological children. Although it is theoretically possible for adolescents to experience enough natal puberty for boys to preserve sperm and girls to harvest eggs, it is rare for natal males to do this, and clinicians say that natal girls categorically reject it. Thus, in effect, when adolescents agree to cross-sex hormones, they or their parents are consenting to lifelong infertility.

Can a young teen understand this? It depends. As 22-year-old trans male Zachary Kerr of Methuen, Mass., recalls about the decision to take testosterone, "I blocked out everything that wasn't good because I wanted it. I was 16. I didn't care."

Other clinicians say that parents must choose for their children, just as they would if a treatment for cancer resulted in permanent infertility. "For some of these kids," says Michele Angello, a psychotherapist and gender specialist in Wayne, Pa., "the outcome is grim if we don't treat." As it is with so many issues these young people face, families and clinicians must recognize that each case is unique and that there are risks on every side. "There is no one right answer," Olson says. "Trans kids throughout life have to decide between bad choices."

More broadly, it is this keen awareness of the challenges that young trans individuals face and the limits of current knowledge that motivate concern on both sides of ongoing debates. Day to day, clinicians are doing their best to navigate between the known and unknown, but answers to at least some key questions may soon be coming. In August 2015 the National Institutes of Health awarded $5.7 million to four major transgender centers for a five-year study of the physical and psychosocial outcomes of treatment for transgender youth.

Ultimately the best course will be to balance the ability to individualize care with caution. "Those of us doing this the longest," Edwards-Leeper says, "feel more concern. Because we see how complex these cases are, and we understand brain development and child and adolescent development. Some newer doctors who just want to advocate for the children can lose sight of the bigger picture."

And both clinicians and families agree that a larger battle of acceptance and tolerance is still being fought. Despite the outpouring of government research funds, media attention and transgender pride in places such as Los Angeles and Seattle, it is important to remember that through great swaths of this country, trans kids face ignorance, blocked pathways and stigma.

Lenessa, a gentle, soft-spoken 14-year-old trans girl from a small town in Texas, came close to becoming a statistic at age 11. From her youngest childhood, she had wanted to be a girl and wear "flowy" dresses, she says, but she was not allowed. While her two brothers roughhoused outside, she would read and sew indoors. The start of puberty was a shock. "I will never forget how horrible it was," she says. "It started to become permanent that I was a boy–becoming a man."

When, with her mother's help, she realized that she was trans and told her family, her father and grandmother rejected her. "Except my mom," she says, "everyone I loved seemed not to want to be with me. That's when I really didn't want to live." To protect her from her suicidal impulses, her mother took her to a psychiatric hospital. For her father, it was "a wake-up call." "I wanted a live child," he says, "not a dead son."

Even with both parents agreeing, finding a way forward was hard. Neither Lenessa's school nor her pediatrician had ever heard of being trans. Long searching led them to Ximena Lopez at the gender clinic at Children's Medical Center Dallas, which is affiliated with the University of Texas Southwestern Medical Center.

Now, at 14, Lenessa is on blockers and, her father says, is flourishing. They have moved to a place where no one knew them before, and the girl who is now Lenessa is about to start high school, wearing the dresses that she loves. She hopes to eventually start hormones and develop a more womanly body. She says she understands the sacrifice she will be making: "It makes me sad when I realize I can't have my own children. But sometimes in life, when you really want something, you have to accept things you don't like."

About the Author

Francine Russo is a veteran journalist specializing in social sciences and relationships. She is author of Love after 50: How to Find It, Enjoy It, and Keep It (Simon and Schuster, 2021).

What Are Puberty Blockers, and How Do They Work?

By Allison Parshall

Adolescence can be a uniquely distressing time for young transgender people, who often experience gender dysphoria: a discrepancy between the sex they were assigned at birth and the gender that matches who they are. During this period, hormone production increases, leading to secondary sexual characteristics such as facial hair and breasts. The irreversible, slow-motion physiological changes can be emotionally and mentally disturbing, leading to depression, social withdrawal, self-harm and a risk of suicide. Hormonal medications called gonadotropin-releasing hormone agonists (GnRHas), often referred to as puberty blockers, temporarily halt the production of sex hormones testosterone, estrogen and progesterone with minimal side effects. They can pause puberty and buy transgender children and their caregivers time to consider their options.

These medications are well studied and have been used safely since the late 1980s to pause puberty in adolescents with gender dysphoria. They have been used routinely for even longer in children who enter puberty too early and in adults with a range of other medical conditions. Puberty-blocking medications are part of a class of hormonal therapies that include birth control pills, treatments for menopause symptoms, treatments for certain kinds of cancer, and more.

But despite the evidence for the safety and efficacy of puberty-delaying treatments, some lawmakers across the U.S. have spread false claims about the drugs and other gender-affirming treatments as part of their efforts to ban or severely restrict access to health care for transgender people. Florida, Idaho, Georgia, Indiana, Kentucky, North Dakota, South

Dakota, West Virginia, Arkansas, Mississippi, Utah, Iowa and Tennessee have banned gender-affirming care for anyone under 18 years old. The American Civil Liberties Union is tracking the status of 122 health care–related anti-LGBTQ+ bills, which disproportionally target transgender youth.

Half of transgender people aged 13 to 24 have seriously considered suicide in the past year, according to a 2023 nationwide survey released on May 1 by the Trevor Project, a nonprofit focused on LGBTQ+ suicide prevention. Gender-affirming hormone therapy can decrease this risk. A recent study in the *New England Journal of Medicine*, for example, showed that hormone therapy significantly decreased symptoms of depression and anxiety in transgender youth. Another study found that transgender teenagers who received gender-affirming care were 73 percent less likely to self-harm or have suicidal thoughts than those who didn't.

Medication that pauses puberty, specifically, has the power to prevent a mental health crisis, making the treatment a "profoundly meaningful intervention" for a young person and their family, says Meredithe McNamara, an adolescent medicine physician at the Yale School of Medicine. "Puberty-blocking treatment is probably one of the most compassionate things that a parent can consent to for a transgender child." It allows transgender children and their families the opportunity to weigh their options carefully, without the constant pressure of physical changes, she says.

Puberty has a long natural window, which typically occurs between eight and 14 years of age and lasts from two to five years. Blockers are usually prescribed once puberty has already begun, and the process involves evaluations by multiple doctors, including mental health practitioners, explains Stephen Rosenthal, a member of the board of directors at the World Professional Association for Transgender Health and a pediatric endocrinologist at the University of California, San Francisco, Benioff Children's Hospitals.

"Most people, within a year [of receiving puberty blockers], decide whether or not they're going to continue to transition," says Vin Tangpricha, an adult endocrinologist at Emory University Hospital and Emory University Hospital Midtown and a co-author of some of the foremost clinical guidelines for treating gender dysphoria in the U.S. and worldwide. "You can't have someone on puberty blockers for a prolonged time." If a teen decides not to transition and stops taking puberty blockers, the hormones their body produces on its own will cause puberty to resume. If they decide to move forward with a medical gender transition, they may take some combination of hormones–estrogen for feminizing effects or testosterone for masculinizing effects–to experience puberty that aligns with their gender.

Teens who had access to puberty blockers and hormone therapy require fewer gender-affirming surgeries as adults. The World Professional Association for Transgender Health's latest standards of care do not specify rigid age limits for gender-affirming surgeries; instead they encourage providers to assess the needs of individual patients. Gender-affirming surgeries are not common among those under age 18 and are usually limited to "top surgery," or a mastectomy. Breast reduction surgery is also one of the most common forms of plastic surgery in cisgender teenagers.

At every stage, the adolescents, their families and their doctors monitor their development. Each step of their transition is considered independently and carefully by the young people and their families, McNamara says.

"These puberty-pausing medications are widely used in many different populations and safely so," McNamara says. GnRHas are also used in adolescents to treat endometriosis, a condition in which the cells lining the uterus grow in other parts of the body. These hormonal drugs have provided solutions to a number of hard-to-treat conditions. They adjust hormone levels for people with prostate and breast cancer, pause menstruation for those undergoing chemotherapy and help with in vitro fertilization.

This host of beneficial clinical uses and data, stretching back to the 1980s, shows that GnRHas are not an experimental treatment, as they are sometimes mischaracterized, says Simona Giordano, a bioethicist at the University of Manchester in England. Among patients who have received the treatment, studies have documented vanishingly small regret rates and minimal side effects, as well as benefits to mental and social health.

"From an ethical and a legal perspective, this is a benign medication," Giordano says. She is puzzled by the extra scrutiny these treatments receive, considering their benefits and limited risks. "There are no sound clinical, ethical or legal reasons for denying them to those in need," she says.

Like any medication, GnRHas carry the potential for adverse effects. GnRHas, when used as puberty blockers or for endometriosis, are known to limit the buildup of bone mineral density, raising concerns about bone fractures. But bone density often recovers after sex hormones are reintroduced. The impacts on bone health depend on many factors, such as when someone started taking GnRHas, how long they stayed on the medication, what their sex at birth was and what sex hormones they will go on to take afterward.

But these bone density scores might not tell the full story of a person's long-term health, McNamara explains. An individual's bone density is evaluated on a broader population average–data that might not be representative of transgender people, who often have lower bone density than their cisgender peers to begin with. Transgender people–especially transgender women–are more likely to have lower bone density, whether or not they used puberty blockers. This is potentially because of the social stressors of being transgender, such as social isolation, exclusion from some physical activities and a high prevalence of restrictive eating.

"The bright side of this whole story is that fractures do not appear to be increased [by GnRHas]. That's what we really care about," Tangpricha says. The treatment "hasn't translated to really bad health outcomes." Meanwhile the increased rates of suicide among those who do not receive gender-affirming care is well documented.

"I think the patients and their families have to weigh the risk of having lower bone density versus a gender issue that's not properly treated," Tangpricha says.

The families that McNamara and Rosenthal work with are aware of the potential risks and benefits of puberty blockers. "We [physicians] are honest acknowledgers of the uncertainty to our patients and their parents, who then make informed consent decisions," McNamara says. Caregivers must weigh any concerns against the lifelong risks of not receiving the care, such as depression and suicidality, and the need for future surgeries, she says. "These are private decisions that parents make for their children's well-being. And the conversations had in these private settings are thorough and exhaustive and iterative," she adds.

To McNamara, the widespread attempts to take these decisions out of families' hands by banning care for transgender youth is a clear indication that the goal is not to protect the health of children, as proponents claim. "These bans did not come from a public outcry about concern for trans youth," she says.

Transgender health care bans are increasingly expanding beyond restrictions for minors. Last month an emergency rule by Missouri's state attorney general placed new, onerous restrictions on adults seeking gender-affirming care, including blocking people diagnosed with autism and depression from accessing it. Nearly one in four transgender people are autistic, compared with one in 20 cisgender people, and depression is a common outcome of gender dysphoria. A state judge temporarily blocked the order hours before it was set to take effect last Thursday.

"Politicians deciding what doctors can do puts doctors, not only patients, in a really difficult situation ... of not serving the best interests of the patients," Giordano says. "'Alarming' is, I think, the right word."

About the Author

Allison Parshall is associate editor for mind and brain at Scientific American *and she writes the weekly online Science Quizzes. As a multimedia journalist, she contributes to* Scientific American's *podcast* Science Quickly. *Parshall's work has also appeared in* Quanta Magazine *and Inverse. She graduated from New York University's Arthur L. Carter Journalism Institute with a master's degree in science, health and environmental reporting. She has a bachelor's degree in psychology from Georgetown University.*

Section 2: Gender Expression

When Real Life Is Hostile, LGBTQ+ Gamers Find Friendship Online

By Shannon Liao

When Texas-based fitness instructor Fabby Garza came out as transgender, the first friends she told were those she'd made playing online games. She waited three more years before she started presenting as feminine in the real world. "Once I finally came out, I had to change the way I lived my life. Taking the bus suddenly became incredibly dangerous. I would get harassed and had strange men follow me off the bus, trying to coerce me into having sex with them," Garza says. "But when I got home and played Final Fantasy XIV or Overwatch or Fortnite with friends, they used my name and pronouns. They allowed me to be myself in a place that was actively hostile toward me."

Many gamers with a marginalized sexual orientation or gender identity use the gaming world to express themselves freely despite real-life hostile environments. This is especially common for people in jurisdictions that have adopted or are considering anti-LGBTQ+ legislation. These gamers defy the American stereotype of the white male player—also presumed to be heterosexual and cisgender—whose tastes the video game industry had historically catered to. A recent report from the LGBTQ+ advocacy organization GLAAD found that nearly one in five heavy gamers (those who spend 10 or more hours a week playing) is LGBTQ+. That's higher than previous results; a 2020 Nielsen survey found that 10 percent of such highly engaged gamers were LGBTQ+.

The GLAAD survey reports that LGBTQ+ gamers are 11 percent more likely than straight, cisgender players to use gaming to "escape from difficult situations in the real world" and 24 percent more likely to use it to get through "tough times." A majority (66 percent) of these respondents said gaming lets them express themselves in a way they're not comfortable with doing in the real world. That includes coming out as LGBTQ+, which nearly a dozen people interviewed for this story said that gaming has helped them do.

"A way to think of games is less of escapism and more as 'embrace-ism'—that is, finding people who will embrace you fully and fulfill the needs that you cannot fulfill in other areas of your life," says Karen Schrier, a games professor at Marist College, who has written two books on the subject. "They are also civic communities, just like the town hall, coffee shop [or] school or religious center."

Digital environments have been LGBTQ+ havens since at least the early 1990s, when online chat rooms became a way to build community and coordinate activist events to raise awareness about AIDS. Similarly, games offer a way for LGBTQ+ players to reach others who may not live nearby, according to Cody Mejeur, an assistant professor of games studies at the University at Buffalo—something they experienced firsthand. "I grew up in a conservative part of the Midwest, in a community where being queer or trans was shunned," Mejeur says. "Religious trauma and conversion trauma were common. In that setting, I had to hide who I was the vast majority of the time and only felt safe expressing myself more openly online."

Gaming also provides a playful way to test what it's like to live as a person of a different gender. Garza says she could explore her identity by playing indie games such as Butterfly Soup, about gay girls who play baseball and fall in love, and One Night, Hot Springs, in which a trans woman visits a hot spring in Japan. Garza could also role-play as an android who develops intimate relationships with other trans women. "The cyberpunk trans erotica game Hardcoded helped me finally come to terms with who I am and what I wanted for the rest of my life," she says.

LGBTQ+ identities aren't just represented in small indie games. Blockbuster games and gaming platforms can also encourage player expression. Roblox, an online platform with 70 million daily players, found in a report on Gen Z users that respondents who identified as LGBTQ+ were more likely to have become comfortable dressing their avatars in a gender-fluid way in 2023. "Growing up as a closeted gay child, virtual worlds and gaming platforms like Roblox created spaces where it didn't matter to anyone who I was or what I looked like," says Samuel Jordan, a 24-year-old who runs a successful fashion business in Roblox. "I was free to explore expressing myself in whatever way I felt comfortable, without fear of real-world judgment. I came out as gay for the first time while on Roblox, which later gave me the confidence to do so in my personal life."

Jordan lives in Florida, where it has been "disheartening to live through" the anti-LGBTQ+ legislation that state leaders have pushed–including a law that prevents educators from teaching children in kindergarten through third grade about gender or sexual identity. "Our governor has chosen to broadcast a message of hatred, otherism and intolerance in a quest to fuel his run for the president of the United States," Jordan says, referring to Florida governor Ron DeSantis's now suspended campaign.

Although harassment and homophobia are also prevalent in many online communities, Mejeur points out that avoiding bigots can be simpler online than in real life: "I could just block a bully or load into a different game to get away from them, and that wasn't always possible at school or church or another in-person venue." They note that even in games with communities that have notoriously homophobic reputations, such as Call of Duty or World of Warcraft (both franchises that Mejeur loves), LGBTQ+ players still find each other.

In 2019 Bo Ruberg, a game studies professor at the University of California, Irvine, published a book entitled *Video Games Have Always Been Queer*, which argues that the LGBTQ+ community can carve out supportive spaces in online games despite hostility. "For queer and transgender people who are experiencing increasing societal and political discrimination today, video games don't offer an escape," Ruberg says. "But they do offer a chance to feel happiness or explore new realities while [people are] still living within the very real and often dangerous reality that surrounds them."

Ruberg wasn't surprised by the GLAAD survey results but says that those statistics may have thrown other people for a loop. "People from outside games (and often more mainstream gamers) tend to think that video games have no place for queer people," Ruberg says. "But we're here now, and we've always been here!"

About the Author

Shannon Liao is a video games journalist and deputy gaming editor at Inverse. She's interested in the ways in which we play and how video games affect the brain. She previously ran her own gaming newsletter, Updater, and was a staff writer at the Washington Post, where she broke industry scoops on business and technology. She has also been a tech and culture reporter at CNN and the Verge and has moderated panels across the country at events such as South by Southwest, Advertising Week New York, the Game Developers Conference, the Game Devs of Color Expo, and more.

The Disturbing History of Research into Transgender Identity

By Jack Turban

In 1975 psychiatrist Robert Stoller of the University of California, Los Angeles, wrote something bizarre in his textbook on sex and gender. He asserted that people who were assumed to be boys when they were born but whose gender identity or expression did not match that assumption "often have pretty faces, with fine hair, lovely complexions, graceful movements, and–especially–big, piercing, liquid eyes."Based on this observation, he suggested a theoretical model in which transgender girls become transgender because they are especially cute. Society treats them more like girls, he reasoned, and because of this experience, they start to identify as female.

As a physician-scientist, I'm generally of the opinion that knowledge leads to progress. But studies focused on this particular question–those asking what determines someone's gender identity–have led us down some strange and dangerous paths. Researchers in this area appear to be in search of some objective truth, but the science is rooted in a subjective assumption: that we need to know what makes someone transgender so that they can be "fixed." As a result, scientists have relentlessly pursued such questions, launching studies that promoted ideas that could hurt transgender children and their families.

Stoller's observations motivated many of the psychological theories behind what makes people transgender. In 1993 a group of researchers at the Clarke Institute of Psychiatry in Toronto set out to test his hypothesis that beauty and what was then called "gender identity disorder"were linked. They recruited 17 birth-assigned boys with the diagnosis and 17 birth-assigned boys without it, all around the age of eight. The researchers then took headshots of the children and showed them to 36 college students. The students were asked to rate the youngsters' physical appearance on a scale from one to five with categories such as "attractive," "handsome" and "beautiful." In the end, the college students found the children with "gender identity disorder" to be "prettier" than the cisgender boys. The findings seem to suggest Stoller was right: perhaps, because of their appearance, people treated the youngsters in the former group more like girls, and consequently, they became transgender. Though as the authors mention later in the paper, an equally plausible theory is that these children could have altered their appearance (long hair, et cetera) in ways that matched their identity, leading the college students to associate them with more feminine descriptions such as "pretty."

A few years later, researchers revived this line of investigation, using the headshots of young birth-assigned girls with "gender identity disorder." A group of college students again rated how "ugly" or "pretty" these children appeared, compared with cisgender girls. The children with "gender identity disorder" were rated as less beautiful, prompting the researchers to suggest that they may have been treated more like boys and thus identified as male. It seems more likely that these children simply cut their hair shorter, so the participants attached more masculine words to them. In the end, the study didn't reveal much about what makes someone transgender, but it did promote an offensive theory with the potential to diminish the self-esteem of vulnerable transgender youth.

Researchers also studied the parents of such children. Psychiatry has long been enamored with the theory of mothers harming the development of their children (for example, the refrigerator mother theory posited that autism was caused by a lack of maternal warmth). These studies similarly asked if perhaps parents were to "blame" for their kids' gender identity. In one paper, researchers assessed whether the mothers of children with "gender identity disorder" had more symptoms of either depression or a condition called borderline personality disorder.

They found these mothers had more symptoms of both. Sounds convincing, right? Children must become transgender because their mothers are mentally ill.

What the researchers failed to discuss was that the mothers' symptoms could easily have been caused by the way society treated their children. The subscale of borderline personality disorder that was higher among them was "interpersonal conflict." You don't need to be the parent of a transgender child to imagine that raising your kid in an unaccepting community could create substantial conflict.

In another study, researchers noted that parents of children with "gender identity disorder" did not place strong limits on stereotypically gender atypical behaviors such as birth-assigned boys playing with dolls or birth-assigned girls playing with blocks or transportation toys. Perhaps this was the cause of the "problem"? If these parents had simply cracked down on this behavior early on—ripped the Barbie out of their toddler's hands, say—they may have prevented it, the authors posited. The more likely explanation is that it's difficult to take a doll away from a child who desperately wants to play with it. And that doing so makes them sad and impacts their self-esteem.

In each case, researchers were hyperfocused on finding a problem with either the kids or their parents. But in the end, these scientists failed to establish one. They seemed less interested in a vital reframing: perhaps the issue was not the children's identity but the way society treated them. Instead of supporting these kids, the researchers labeled them unattractive or painted their parents as mentally unstable.

These theories on the origins of gender identity have only added to the misguided, and increasingly illegal, calls for "therapies" designed to make transgender people cisgender. The logic of so-called gender identity conversion therapy is that if the environment is the cause, then we can simply alter the environment to nip things in the bud. Most of the "conversion" manuals have not been released to the public, but in 2002 a psychologist at Columbia University published "Gender Identity Disorder in Young Boys: A Parent and Peer-Based Protocol," which included parenting techniques such as "letting go of [the] boy by [the] mother, "forcing the child to play with same-sex friends, and removing the youngster from stereotypically gender-atypical activities such as gymnastics or ballet. Notably, a recent study my colleagues and I conducted showed that attempts to change a child's gender identity from transgender to cisgender are associated with greater odds of attempting suicide. Several U.S. states have banned conversion therapy, but in much of the U.S., these practices continue.

Similar research into the psychological causes of transgender identity continues even today. A physician at Brown University recently conducted an anonymous survey of respondents recruited via Web sites for parents who believe peer pressure and online influences have made their children transgender. The survey essentially asked the parents if they thought the Internet made their children trans, and the parents, not surprisingly, given that they were visiting Web sites about this idea, answered yes. Conservative media latched onto the study, suggesting that transgender children are really just confused kids tricked into being transgender after reading something on Reddit. The implication is that we need to take these kids away from supportive online LGBTQ communities so that they can be made cisgender again. Reading through this literature, we need to ask ourselves some questions: What is the reason for this research? What does it hope to accomplish? The tireless search reveals a thinly veiled dogma: that being transgender is a pathology to be fixed. This belief not only harms transgender people but also undermines good science.

What good science shows us is that when we accept transgender people, they thrive. Instead of trying to figure out what went "wrong," we should be investing our time and energy into advocating for nondiscrimination laws, increasing access to health care and raising transgender voices in the media, so society realizes that they are vital members of our communities. Maybe Stoller was right when he noted that those children were exceptional. It's time we celebrate that and move on.

About the Author

Jack Turban is a fellow in child and adolescent psychiatry at the Stanford University School of Medicine, where he researches the mental health of transgender youth. His writing has appeared in the New York Times, *the* Washington Post, *the* Los Angeles Times, *and more. Follow him on Twitter@jack_turban.*

Sex and Gender Map onto Different Brain Networks in Children

By Allison Parshall

A new brain-imaging study of young adolescents has shown that sex and gender map onto different brain networks. The findings, published on Friday in *Science Advances*, demonstrate the importance of considering the social impact of gender in neuroscience research rather than conflating it with physiological sex.

"Moving forward, we really need to consider both sex and gender separately if we want to better understand the brain," said study co-author Elvisha Dhamala, a neuroscientist at the Feinstein Institutes for Medical Research, in a recent press conference.

Physiological sex is largely determined by chromosomes, genes, hormones and other biological systems. On top of that, cultural ideas about what it means to be, for example, a man, woman or nonbinary person–what we call gender–also play a critical role shaping people's life and behavior. Scientists understand sex and gender to be related yet distinct concepts, but they are often conflated in neuroscience research. This means that differences between the brains of people who are assigned male or female at birth are often taken as reflections of biological differences when they could very well be the result of how each group is treated based on cultural expectations.

"The influence of being treated as a woman or as a man in our society is ignored" in neuroscience research, says Lara M. Wierenga, a neuroscientist who studies gender differences in brain development at Leiden University in the Netherlands and was not involved in the new research. "But we also know that the brain is very plastic, very open to experiences," which can differ greatly between people assigned female or male at birth, she says.

For the new study, Dhamala's team wanted to know what the field might be missing by ignoring the social impact of gender. The researchers worked with data from a large and ongoing longitudinal study of U.S. adolescents to compare brain scan data with questionnaire responses about the participants' sex and gender from them and their parents.

While the researchers expected sex to be associated with differences in activity in certain brain networks, beyond that, "we had no idea whether or not [gender] would map onto the brain and also no idea *where* it would map onto the brain," Dhamala says.

The study researchers analyzed functional magnetic resonance imaging (fMRI) data from 4,757 children aged nine or 10 years old. The fMRI scanner captured "resting-state" activity across different brain regions that occurs when someone is awake but not engaged in a specific task. The young participants had also been asked four questions about their feelings about their gender (such as "How much do you feel like a boy?"), and their parents had been asked 12 questions about how their child talked about their gender and how they engaged in play activities that are stereotypically "for boys" or "for girls."

The researchers fed the brain-scan data, along with information about each participant's sex, into a machine-learning model, which learned to pick out subtle differences in the activity of certain regions of the brain between the male and female groups. Then they tested the model on data it had not yet seen by asking it to predict participants' sex based on their brain scans, which it accomplished with 77 percent accuracy.

Next, the researchers went on to train another machine-learning model to make predictions from the preteens' and parents' reports about gender. But because sex and gender are so strongly related to each other, the brain networks associated with each largely overlapped. To bring gender into clearer view, the team analyzed the participants' gender variation separately by sex. This showed how and where brain activity differed between people who had been assigned the same sex at birth but had varying feelings and expression of their gender.

Finally, the researchers compared the networks associated with gender differences with those associated with sex differences. They found that while there was some overlap, these groups of networks were largely different from one another, though this difference was only statistically significant for the parent-reported gender data, not the self-reports. (The study authors think the self-report questionnaire was not sensitive enough to capture differences in how children think and feel about their gender.)

The brain networks unique to sex but not gender included networks with more well-defined roles in the brain, such as the visual network and motor network. Conversely, the networks that showed gender but not sex differences were more dispersed throughout the brain. It's too soon to draw conclusions about why some networks were associated with sex and not gender and vice versa, Dhamala says: "We have no idea right now" if those differences relate to differences in behavior.

"This is really the first time that it's shown in such a large dataset that not only sex but also gender is related to the way the brain is wired," Wierenga says. "The expectations that we have [based on gender], they do matter." This is important to understand because gender-related differences in the brain could impact how psychiatric disorders manifest across the gender spectrum, especially those that are underdiagnosed in people who were assigned female at birth (such as attention-deficit hyperactivity disorder, or ADHD) or who were assigned male (such as anxiety and mood disorders), Wierenga says.

Because the research was only done in children, it's also not clear whether gender would map onto the brain differently from sex in adults, though Wierenga says she expects that this pattern would hold.

Dhamala's team plans to rerun similar analyses on the same group of children as they grow. "These are still very young kids. And as they go through adolescence and into adulthood, their brain networks and their functional connectivity is going to be changing," she says. In the meantime, the researchers say, other teams could begin testing gender as well as sex in their research to yield a clearer picture of brain-based differences throughout life.

About the Author

Allison Parshall is associate editor for mind and brain at Scientific American *and she writes the weekly online Science Quizzes. As a multimedia journalist, she contributes to* Scientific American's *podcast* Science Quickly. *Parshall's work has also appeared in* Quanta Magazine *and Inverse. She graduated from New York University's Arthur L. Carter Journalism Institute with a master's degree in science, health and environmental reporting. She has a bachelor's degree in psychology from Georgetown University.*

There Are No Such Things as Gendered Emotions

By Pragya Agarwal

A couple of years ago I was at the ophthalmologist with my six-year-old daughter. The optician asked me more than once, "Why has she been frowning all the time? Why is she so serious?"

I cannot know how much my child's being a girl shaped the optician's thoughts about her emotional state. But I know from my research on the gendering of emotions that people start expecting women and girls to show nurturing and positive expressions early. A different group of researchers analyzed more than 16,000 yearbook photographs of students from kindergarten to college, as well as school faculty and staff. The children showed no significant difference in smiling until age eight or nine, but then the gap started to widen, with girls smiling much more than boys. The difference between girls and boys peaked by the time the students were 14 years old, with girls smiling more frequently and more broadly than boys, and this contrast remained consistent over adulthood.

We may see such results because as children grow older, they become more aware of societal expectations related to gender roles. These expectations could come from peer groups or be imposed on them by parents, teachers or, in the case of the yearbook photos, photographers, both implicitly and explicitly. People may also internalize gender roles portrayed in film and media, where smiling is perceived as more feminine (smiling women are considered more pleasant and friendly) and seriousness is seen as a characteristic of masculinity.

In a different study in which teachers reported their students' emotional expressions, girls were described as having more "peaceful," "calm" and "neutral" expressions (all positive but passive emotions involving little agency), whereas boys showed more "surprise," "curiosity," "anger" and "frustration" (more agentic, or proactive, emotions). It is a widely held misconception that girls are better than boys at regulating their emotions: no neuroscience studies have shown that self-regulatory mechanisms are more developed or active in girls than they are in boys.

Society expects brown women to be more acquiescent and perceives Black women who aren't acquiescent as angry. As a mixed-race girl, my child is likely to encounter some of these stereotypes. A study of American storybooks showed that Hispanic and Latino characters display happiness proportionally more than other characters, whereas white American characters have the space to show displeasure, aligning with the individualistic values of many Western cultures. Children may receive specific messages about emotions while reading storybooks—not only gendered but also culture-specific.

These emotional stereotypes present a double bind for parents hoping to help their children develop emotional intelligence and autonomy. Very early on, children learn to modulate their emotions in line with societal norms they pick up from their peers and caregivers. Regularly suppressing our emotions can massively affect our mental and physical health. Emotional expectations and the offhand comments that children internalize over time harm all kids, irrespective of gender. These expectations can have long-standing negative effects on their sense of self, too. If, however, children do not conform to the behaviors and norms of their membership groups, they may face bullying.

Teaching our children to regulate their emotions is not wrong. Emotional socialization is an important part of parenting to build children's emotional competence and to align them with the values of a particular community. But it is wrong to expect different things from our children based on their gender and race and to minimize or invalidate their emotions based on what we perceive as the correct emotional response. We talk with our children about bodily autonomy; we should also talk about emotional autonomy and how they can better understand and have agency over their own feelings.

Recently I have been reflecting on my relationship with emotions and how I might have endorsed certain expectations through words and actions. According to psychologist John M. Gottman's meta-emotion framework, parents' attitude toward emotions and the way they accept or reject certain ones in themselves affect which emotions they validate in their children.

Many people grew up with very specific emotional rules and model them in their own parenting, consciously or unconsciously. Parents are more likely to validate their child's emotions if they consider those emotions acceptable in general, and they are unlikely to if they believe the cost of expressing the emotion is too high. This cost could be the burden of societal judgment, penalization or ostracization, or it may be an emotional cost the parent pays by having to regulate their own emotions in response.

One study found that mothers were more likely to use emotional language when speaking with four-year-old daughters than with sons that age. Before the start of this experiment, the researchers had observed no difference in emotional understanding and expression between girls andboys, but this changed over the course of the study.

Through the gendered use of language around emotion, children receive a message that certain emotions are more acceptable for girls than for boys and that women talk more about their feelings. Research also shows that parents might react–often unconsciously–in a way that encourages emotional expression in girls but discourages emotional expression in boys. These cues might include ignoring, dismissing or invalidating certain emotions in children: anger in girls and sadness in boys.

So many problems emerge from adults' failure to accept the discomfort that comes with children's emotional expression and the way that leads them to set rules for "good girls" and "good boys."

Anyone might be fearful of people judging them in public and seeing them as bad parents who cannot control or discipline their children. We label emotions as "good" or "bad": happiness is good, anger and sadness are bad. And we may discourage or shy away from any "bad" emotions our children express that might make us feel like we are not being good parents. Even our implicit gestures, facial reactions and tone of voice can give children signals from a young age as to which emotions are acceptable and which we should hide away or suppress.

Marc Brackett, director of the Yale Center for Emotional Intelligence, proposes that parents have to find their "best selves" before they can help their children with extreme emotions. From my standpoint, a better approach would be to stop labeling some emotions as "extreme," avoid setting such fixed bounds around emotional expression and not expect children to all conform to the same template.

If we reflected on the messages we internalized while growing up, we could allow ourselves and our children to sit with the discomfort of such "negative" emotions. Over the years, I have realized that it is not my responsibility as a parent to always protect my children from sadness or anger. Children ought to know that such emotions are part of our everyday life–that it is okay to feel sad, frustrated and angry. It is what we do with these emotions that matters.

Teaching children to understand how they are feeling and learn strategies to tackle their emotions is a way of encouraging their emotional autonomy. It is also important for children to know the correct vocabulary so they can name their emotions for themselves and others.

After our visit to the ophthalmologist, my child wondered, "Mummy, should I have been smiling?" I reminded her that she did not have to fake a smile. But even as I have taught her that she doesn't have to modulate or suppress her emotions for anyone else, I have wondered anxiously how much others will judge her for not conforming and what the cost of that will be. I am not suggesting that we each take individual responsibility for resolving the emotional biases in society that perpetuate and enable gender and racial inequities. But we can all reflect on our internal emotional framework and challenge emotional norms, acknowledging that we might be enforcing some of these arbitrary rules, without even realizing it, through our words and our actions.

About the Author

Pragya Agarwal is a behavioral and data scientist, author of four nonfiction books, a visiting professor of social inequities and injustice at Loughborough University, a fellow at Newnham College, Cambridge University, and a visiting fellow of Black and South Asian history at the University of Oxford. Her latest book is Hysterical: Exploding the Myth of Gendered Emotions *(Canongate, 2022). More at drpragyaagarwal.com and on X: @drpragyaagarwal*

Section 3: Gender and Sports

Sports Celebrate Physical Variation—Until It Challenges Social Norms

By Bethany Brookshire

The Olympics are a celebration of athletic prowess, an event that incidentally highlights the diversity of the human body. Take height for example. Simone Biles, the GOAT, hurtled herself through her Paris 2024 floor routine at 4'8". Meanwhile, on the basketball court, some players seemed to barely reach the waist of the 7'4" French star Victor Wembanyama (that's over 1.5 Simone Bileses).

Height may be the most obvious difference, but there are others. Broad shoulders can make a difference in rugby, weightlifting and swimming. Then there are the ones we can't see: sprinters have more of fast-twitch muscle fibers for short, explosive bursts. Long distance runners have more slow-twitch muscle fibers to go the distance. Genetic tweaks could increase some athletes red blood cell count–a definite advantage for endurance. Some Paris athletes probably had extra vertebrae. Extra ribs. They could help, they could hurt–or they could do nothing at all.

Our bodies are festivals of variation. And in sports, we celebrate those differences–until we don't. In certain sports, people are much more skeptical and far less accepting of variations among women athletes. With all our uniqueness, it seems strange to me that we laud some anatomical variations and are so hostile towards others. What matters is not whether a particular variation is common or rare, but how we perceive it in terms of the societal categories we have made. And because of our perceptions, some athletes end up adored. Others are shamed for some of the very characteristics that could help make them great.

People routinely categorize and put things in boxes, and societal requirements even make us do this to ourselves; check one box for nationality, another for age group. Check a box for race (a social construct and not a biological reality, though the consequences are extremely real). And check yet another for your sex. Make sure you use a number two pencil, and whatever you do, don't mark outside of the box.

How we study the human body is not immune to this box-checking either; anatomists have strived to work out the structure of a "normal" human body, regardless of how "normal" any of us actually are. But in spite of us having an idea of how a body is most likely to look, there are still plenty of ways our bodies can veer out of this "normal" box we've created. The appendix, for example, is only in the expected position (flipped up over the tip of the cecum of the large intestine) 56 percent of the time, meaning almost half of the population has one pointing an unusual way. We're taught that our skeletons, too, have 33 vertebrae, but around 8 percent of people will have 32 or 34 vertebrae instead. While 99 percent of the population has 12 pairs of ribs, a lucky 1 percent has a 13th pair. Another 1 percent has an entire extra lobe of the lung, called an azygos lobe, which even doctors can mistake as an abscess. Another incredible variation that pops up in a mere 0.3 percent of the population, including the famous cross-country skier Eero Mäntyranta, is the ability to produce excessive red blood cell count–which is, of course, very advantageous for endurance sports.

It's easy to see why anatomists, and by extension doctors, might want to establish a "normal" idea of how a human body looks and works; if there ever comes a need to go inside one, it's helpful to know what's likely to be where. But when our anatomical variations intersect with our social ideas of how people should look and behave–especially around the ideas of femininity and masculinity–the unexpected can often be labeled "abnormal." And with "abnormal" comes societal judgement.

For people assigned male at birth, variations in anatomy that enhance their athletic abilities are often deemed impressive, such as wide "wingspans" or a long stride. People with large amounts of those explosive, fast-twitch muscle fibers may pack a powerful punch or hoist a massive clean and jerk. But for people assigned female at birth, some of those same variations are suddenly unfair advantages.

This is especially true when those variations cross over into what people perceive as traits that are "manly." No one complains of the flexibility and strength of female gymnasts–it is merely amazing. A powerful triple axel on the ice is perfectly feminine when done in a skirt. But a powerful punch? A cheetah-fast sprint? Variation is suddenly of deep concern.

In competition, categorizing becomes especially strict. We so desperately want to know who is the best, but we also want to control what "best" really means. For "feminine" sports, such as women's gymnastics or figure skating, the sky is the limit for what these women can do. We praise their perfect builds for their sport and cheer their accomplishments. But for other sports, it seems female athletes can only achieve so much and still retain the approval of their audiences and fellow competitors. One merely needs to look it this Olympics' boxing controversy to see this, but there are many other occasions where female athletes have been shunned or flat-out banned for their naturally occurring "masculine" traits.

This leads us to, of course, hormones. As Rose Eveleth points out in their excellent podcast Tested, female athletes often experience rigorous testing, particularly of their testosterone levels, which must be within specific ranges to compete. But hormone levels are yet another bodily feature that can't be neatly put into a checked box–there is plenty of natural variation, with levels changing throughout lifespans and from person to person. And some people naturally produce more or fewer receptors for those hormones too, affecting how "visible" these chemicals are to cells, regardless of the blood test result. The human body can respond to these naturally occurring hormonal differences in a variety of ways; for example, during male puberty, many kids will have a temporary enlargement of their breast tissue, known as pubertal gynecomastia, in response to swelling hormones. One might think such an occurrence is rare, but it's been found that up to 70 percent of kids assigned male at birth will experience this tissue enlargement–and the stigma and bullying that goes with it–even though it can statistically be considered as an anatomical "norm."

Hormones are one of the major check boxes where our desire for entertaining, "fair" competition and social ideas of what "female" *should* be clash against the variability of nature. But our competitive sporting categorization of what "female" is–of how much testosterone they're naturally allowed to produce, of how much their physicality is allowed to deviate from what's considered the "normal" female body–this categorization is yet another one that we have created. A categorization that considers only some anatomical variations passable as female, and others strictly not.

The difference isn't in which parts of anatomy or physiology are too large, too small, too high, or too low, too wide or too narrow, too much or too little. People assigned female at birth exist well outside either end of the narrow biochemical definitions we have set. The difference instead is in what people perceive: what they believe female athletes should be like, how well athletes assigned female at birth should perform.

These narrow definitions not only harm athletes, but sport itself; when Michael Phelps blows every other swimmer out of the water in a race, we do not think twice about it being his natural gifts (his variations) as an athlete. But when a female runner or boxer does the same, suddenly people begin to jump to conclusions about how "female" they really are.

The vast array of bodies at the Olympics shows there is no one way an athlete looks. Beholding our amazing variability–and learning a little about our anatomy–makes it clear that acceptance of some variation, and punishment of others, is much more about society than it is about any athlete at all.

About the Author

Bethany Brookshire is an award-winning science journalist and author of the book Pests: How Humans Create Animal Villains *(Ecco, 2022). Her work has appeared in* Scientific American, *the* New York Times, *the* Washington Post, *the* Atlantic *and other outlets.*

Hormone Levels Are Being Used to Discriminate against Female Athletes

By Grace Huckins

In February 2016 Dutee Chand became the best woman sprinter in India. The record she set on an indoor track in Qatar during a qualifying heat stands as the fastest time an Indian woman has ever achieved in the 60-meter race, and she soon became the first Indian woman in decades to race the 100 meters at the Olympics. Just a year earlier, however, Chand had faced the possibility of never again running competitively.

In 2014, as Chand was making her mark on the junior-level track world, the Athletics Federation of India (AFI), with the support of its international parent body World Athletics, barred her from competing in women's events because of atypically high levels of testosterone occurring naturally in her body. (There is no evidence Chand ever took banned substances to alter her hormones.) According to the AFI, which runs India's track-and-field competitions, her higher-than-average testosterone level gave her physical advantages enjoyed by male athletes. Chand disputed the idea that this hyperandrogenism—an elevated level of androgens, the class of hormones that includes testosterone—made her more like a male sprinter than a female one, and in 2015 the Court of Arbitration for Sport agreed with her. It determined that World Athletics, which sets the rules governing international track-and-field competitions, had not presented enough scientific evidence to defend its claims—and Chand could run again.

But World Athletics now contends that it has found an adequate scientific basis for barring women with high testosterone from competing in races between 400 meters and one mile unless they take medication to lower their testosterone levels or opt to compete against men. This policy does not apply to Chand, because she runs shorter distances, but it could end the athletic dreams of Mokgadi

Caster Semenya, an Olympic gold medalist and a hero in her home country of South Africa. In 2019 the Court of Arbitration for Sport accepted World Athletics' argument, and the Swiss Supreme Court upheld this decision in September 2020. Rather than undergo medically unnecessary treatment to suppress her testosterone levels, Semenya has decided to compete only in the 200-meter race, an event without limits on testosterone levels, at the 2021 Tokyo Olympics.

This sequence of controversial decisions has prompted a public debate about fairness and discrimination in sports. Throughout the Olympics' modern history, rules about who counts as a woman have shifted as the scientific understanding of sex has progressed. Disqualifying athletes on the basis of natural testosterone levels is one of the last legal forms of discrimination in sports.

As an interdisciplinary scholar trained in both biology and gender studies, I have examined the ways in which scientists take social categories such as "woman" and "man" and attempt to turn them into fundamental truths. For as long as scientists have been trying to figure out the biological basis of sex and gender, nature has presented divergences from their theories. ("Sex" refers to biological characteristics; "gender" refers to social roles and identification.)

Most men have XY chromosomes and developed testicles in utero that, later in life, secrete relatively high amounts of testosterone into their bloodstreams. In contrast, most women have XX chromosomes, which drives the production of ovaries and lower levels of testosterone. Some women, however, have XY chromosomes as well as external female anatomy; these women are affected by the World Athletics policy. Such attributes reflecting variation beyond the rigid male/female binary are known as intersex traits.

According to interAct, an intersex advocacy organization, 1.7 percent of the population may be intersex, although many never realize it. And they may be overrepresented in the world of elite sports: in its published decision, the Court of Arbitration for Sport repeatedly referenced the statistic that among elite athletes, women with XY chromosomes are far more common than they are in the general population.

It seems, then, that intersex women may have an edge in athletic competitions. But so, too, do athletes with natural advantages such as, say, height in basketball tournaments. The important question here is not whether some sex traits can confer athletic advantages but whether those advantages are so meaningful and so incontrovertible that they should prevent a woman athlete such as Semenya from competing against other women.

Chromosomes and Hormones

Sex has never been a simple binary. Nevertheless, Olympic regulators have tried for decades to apply overly simplistic rules to this messy reality. From the 1960s until the 1990s dozens of women were singled out and even disqualified because of their chromosomes. The first was Ewa Kłobukowska, who was deemed a woman based on genital examination in 1966 but was disqualified from the 1968 Olympics because of her XY chromosomal makeup. Kłobukowska's story is not so surprising: Some intersex women are anatomically so similar to other women that they never discover their XY chromosomal makeup.

Chromosomal testing thus disqualified some people who had every trait of the female sex except for XX chromosomes. This contradiction, coupled with the invasiveness of some testing and the dire social consequences for those who failed the tests, eventually led the International Olympic Committee to abandon sex testing in the 1990s. But its concern about ensuring the apparent fairness of women's competitions did not disappear, and it reserved for itself the option to test people on a case-by-case basis. Recent cases of sex testing have focused not on chromosomes but on an aspect of sex ostensibly more related to athletic ability: testosterone levels.

Athletes have been using artificial testosterone since at least the 1950s in the hopes of improving their performance, but until the 1990s the medical community did not hold that the link between supplemental testosterone and athletic ability had adequate scientific support. That might have influenced the International Olympic Committee's choice not to use testosterone levels in its sex-verification era. The paradigm changed after 1996, when a study demonstrated that testosterone supplementation, in combination with weight training, could increase both muscle size and strength in men.

Since then, endocrinologists have greatly expanded their understanding of the relation between testosterone and muscle mass. The evidence shows that testosterone both increases the number of muscle cells that the body produces and enhances muscle size. There is some evidence that testosterone may also influence athletic ability through other mechanisms. In one experiment, men who took high levels of testosterone (but not those who took lower levels) had increased levels of hemoglobin in their bloodstreams, a change that allows blood to carry more oxygen to the rest of the body. Testosterone could also exert influence on bone mass because low testosterone levels, much like low estrogen levels, are correlated with osteoporosis, and both hormones have a role in maintaining bone structure.

In fact, androgens ("male" hormones, including testosterone) and estrogens ("female" hormones) are much more tightly linked than most people imagine. For starters, everyone naturally produces both hormones. And all naturally occurring estrogen in humans was once testosterone, transformed into estrogen by the enzyme aromatase. Scientists debate how much of a given hormone is "normal" and how those levels should be measured—one recent study even concluded that "normal" testosterone levels for women should be adjusted to better accommodate female athletes. And men's and women's estrogen levels can actually overlap, especially during some phases of the menstrual cycle. Even so, testosterone levels do vary considerably between men and women: younger men's levels tend to range between 10 and 40 nanomoles per liter of blood, whereas women's levels tend to range between 0.5 and 3 nmol/L.

Taken together, the available evidence—the gap in between most men's and women's testosterone levels, the established connection between testosterone doping and increased muscle mass, and the approximately 10 percent advantage that elite men have over elite women in track events—seems to imply that women with high testosterone levels will run like men. Nevertheless in Chand's case, the Court of Arbitration for Sport found that she could not be banned from competition, because there was not yet any direct evidence of the relation between natural testosterone levels and athletic ability in elite women.

The court decided differently in Semenya's case four years later, partly because it believed that such evidence had been produced. Stéphane Bermon, head of World Athletics' scientific team, had recently published a paper that analyzed data from two international athletics competitions and found that women with higher levels of testosterone performed better, on average, than women with lower levels. Because this study is based on real-world data from elite female runners, it arguably represents the most relevant findings in the hyperandrogenism controversy to date.

I spend some of my research time trawling the scientific literature to find cases of researchers making statistical errors, particularly when their studies pertain to marginalized groups. So I was intrigued to read that a group of scientists had questioned the validity of this key study on the basis of issues with the data. In response to their concerns, Bermon updated the study, and although he still observed some effects, his conclusion was markedly weakened by the correction. When I performed a procedure called correcting for multiple comparisons—a statistical method that takes into account the increased probability of finding at least one false positive when many statistical tests, as opposed to only one, are conducted—on his reported results, these effects disappeared.

This complication does not imply that there is no relation between testosterone and athletic performance in women. What is certainly the case, however, is that far more research is needed before a firm conclusion can be reached.

Supplemental is not Natural

If testosterone taken illegally and testosterone produced naturally had the same impact on all bodies, one would assume that male-typical levels of testosterone necessarily confer a male-typical athletic advantage. But to understand what such studies mean for women like Semenya, we must understand how their bodies work. All the women targeted by World Athletics' policy on testosterone levels are intersex, with a similar set of sex traits: they have XY chromosomes, but their bodies do not respond to androgens in the same way most XY individuals do. Because of the complexity inherent in the function of hormones, it is extremely difficult to determine the precise effect that testosterone will have on these intersex people.

Even if androgens did have a completely typical effect on them, the link between testosterone and athletic ability would remain far more tenuous than it might seem. Taking *supplemental* testosterone may tend to give someone bigger muscles, but that does not automatically imply that a person with *naturally* higher testosterone levels will be better at sports than someone with lower testosterone levels. Even the original, contested version of Bermon's study hints at a nuanced connection: whereas testosterone showed a positive effect on athletic ability for a couple of events, no effect was observed for 16 other events, and the data suggested that higher testosterone levels may be associated with worse performance in several events.

One study of elite Swedish athletes found no association between testosterone and athletic performance, and a recent study of teenage athletes in Australia showed a strong negative correlation between testosterone levels in women and performance. Men, too, do not necessarily gain an enormous advantage from high testosterone levels: almost 17 percent of elite male athletes measured in one study had testosterone levels *below* the typical male range, and nearly 10 percent of them had testosterone levels under 5 nmol/L.

The clear effect of testosterone supplements on the body and the average differences in muscle mass between men and women make it easy to assume that higher testosterone levels automatically confer superior athletic ability regardless of other factors. But the science shows that, at least among elite athletes, the link between testosterone and athletic performance is far from straightforward.

One of the first things a person learns when studying the science of sex and gender is how difficult it is to disentangle biological and social influences. For me, this issue came into stark relief when I studied apparently sex-linked advantages in areas such as spatial ability. Because men tend to experience both higher levels of testosterone and more encouragement in STEM fields than do their female counterparts, it is difficult to determine whether biological or social factors cause these differences. To answer these questions, scientists study people who have high testosterone and do not experience a masculine social environment–that is, women with particular intersex traits–and examine their behavior to differentiate between biological and social causes.

The story gets far more convoluted when we try not only to distinguish between biological and social causes but also to investigate how those factors interact. One fascinating example comes from the work of neuroscientist Melissa Hines, who studied girls with congenital adrenal hyperplasia, a condition in which intersex traits arise in XX females because of unusually high levels of androgens. Hines showed that these girls tend to engage in play behavior seen relatively more often in boys, such as horseplay. More recently, however, she demonstrated that the girls do not necessarily prefer horseplay over dolls: they just do not care about what other girls tend to do. Most young girls will prefer to play with a red ball over a blue ball if they see that other girls are playing only with red balls, but girls with congenital adrenal hyperplasia will happily play with either toy. Testosterone does not make girls more likely to wrestle than to read; it simply changes the extent to which they respond to social cues about gender.

In terms of its effects on behavior, testosterone is thus quite complex: it seems to work together with social cues such that neither factor can be isolated from the other. Although these apparently psychological observations may be irrelevant to the question of athletic ability, even Bermon and his colleagues have suggested that dominance and aggression, long associated with testosterone levels, could have a role in winning races. In one of the only studies that systematically examined the effect of taking testosterone on women's physical ability, those who took high levels of the hormone saw modestly increased muscle mass and dramatically increased strength. The researchers hypothesized that some unmeasured psychological factor allowed their slightly more developed muscles to make extraordinary athletic gains.

But it is also far too simplistic to assume that testosterone causes aggression or competitiveness, even though women might be more likely to enter competitive situations when their testosterone levels are higher, and men who respond more strongly to androgens might be more confident about their chances in competition. In fact, numerous studies have demonstrated that a person's testosterone levels will increase after, rather than before, they have won a competition or otherwise shown dominance, and one 2015 study suggested that this effect might be stronger in women than it is in men. Behavior, which is affected by social norms about men and women, exerts an influence on hormone levels–demonstrating yet again the intricate and perhaps inextricable links between the social and the biological.

When critics argue that intersex women are basically "biological men" who just happen to have clitorises and labia, they are completely neglecting the enormous influences that the categories "men" and "women" have on all of our lives–and on all of our bodies. Testosterone is not some mysterious entity that comes from nowhere to exert a huge influence on our bodies and our minds: it both changes and is changed by gender norms.

Despite being just a single element in a knotty, sometimes circular network of factors that contribute to athletic ability, testosterone is unlikely to be completely irrelevant. Somehow XY women seem likelier to achieve physical feats than XX women. This observation does not imply, however, that intersex women should be forced to compete in the men's category against men, against whom they will surely lose. Arguing that biology instructs us to divide athletes at a threshold of five nanomoles of testosterone per liter of blood, as World Athletics has done, implies that this threshold splits humans into the two fairest, most equal competitive groups possible.

Given that testosterone affects athletic ability in a complex, nonlinear fashion, this suggestion is not supported by the evidence. It would be far more sensible to split basketball into two separate height divisions: no current player in the NBA is shorter than 5'9", whereas both low-testosterone men and low-testosterone women can be extremely successful athletes. Nor is there any cogent reason to identify intersex conditions as conferring unique genetic advantages in a domain such as elite athletics, where a variety of unusual traits lead to success. Why should swimmer Michael Phelps's low lactic acid production (which helps stave off muscle fatigue) or the late NBA player Manute Bol's uncommon height be rewarded while Semenya's somewhat higher testosterone level is disqualifying?

If biology cannot give us a firm basis for dividing athletes into two distinct categories, we might wonder why we have men's and women's divisions at all. Although testosterone levels might not divide all of humanity neatly into better and worse athletes, it is the case that, at the most elite level, men outperform women in sports such as track. Making sports coed and thus de facto barring women from Olympic races would not be intrinsically unfair–after all, plenty of groups of people, such as those with poor cardiovascular health, can never dream of becoming elite runners–but it would be regrettable. We would lose women such as sprinter Allyson Felix, swimmer Katie Ledecky and the extraordinary U.S. women's soccer squad, all of whom inspire countless young women.

Biology alone is too limited a tool to tell us how to divide up the athletic field—but it can help us gain a greater understanding of natural human variation. Particularly in a domain as convoluted and controversial as sex and gender, science often uncovers more ambiguity than it resolves. And if science does not inform the issue of intersex women in sports, we can still revert to the values of diversity, inclusion and acceptance that make elite women's sports so extraordinary in the first place.

About the Author

Grace Huckins is a doctoral student in neuroscience at Stanford University and a graduate of the master's programs in neuroscience and women's studies at the University of Oxford.

The Long History of Sex Testing in the Olympics and Other Elite Sports

By Rachel Feltman, Fonda Mwangi & Jeffery DelViscio

Rachel Feltman: There have been a lot of headlines in recent years about transgender athletes. But this isn't actually the first time debates over biological sex have caused controversy and exclusion in the sports world.

Even athletes who identify with the sex they were assigned at birth, meaning people with XX chromosomes who were assigned female at birth and identify as women today, can find themselves banned from elite competition on the basis of their biology.

For *Scientific American's Science Quickly*, I'm Rachel Feltman. Today I'm talking to award-winning reporter and writer Rose Eveleth. They're the creator and host of a new series called *Tested,* co-produced by CBC Podcasts and NPR's *Embedded.*

Tested follows the surprising 100-year history of sex testing in elite sports, which has culminated in some shocking modern policies.

So, Rose, for listeners who aren't familiar with your work, I would love to hear a little bit more about how you came to this story.

Rose Eveleth: I was an intern in the ye olde days of *Scientific American.*

Feltman: As was I! What a time.

Eveleth: Yeah, in the blog minds of early science Internet. But so I was an intern at *Scientific American*, and I was looking for something to write about, and I had been writing a lot about prosthetics because, you know, when you're an intern you say yes to literally anything anyone gives you to write.

And as I was looking for something to write about, I came across the story of Oscar Pistorius, who is a South African man who is a double amputee and who, at the time, was actually trying to race against able-bodied runners, and this was a big controversy because, you know, there was this question of, "Does he have an unfair advantage because his legs are so light and he might actually be able to run faster than someone who has full legs?" And I found that super interesting 'cause I was like, okay, what do we mean when we say an "unfair advantage" in sports? And it seems a little bit counterintuitive, perhaps, to think that, like, a double amputee has an unfair advantage in running.

Feltman: Right.

Eveleth: Like, that's sort of an interesting, like, you know, thing to think about. And also, how would you even test that? And so I was reading about that, and I came across some other precedent about a different South African runner named Caster Semenya, who in 2009 broke onto the world stage and was very publicly questioned about her sex and was told that she also had an unfair advantage because of her body's biology. And I had heard about Caster when this all happened in 2009, but, like, I didn't really follow it 'cause honestly I remember seeing the headlines and being like, "What? Like, this doesn't make any sense." But in, I think it was 2012, I started really researching it, and I was like, "Whoa, there's this really long history. There's 100 years of sort of sex-testing policies." And then, as I've been following it, those policies have changed over time and are still active.

Feltman: So looking back at the Olympics specifically, since 'tis the season, what did you learn about how these questions sort of, like, first arose?

Eveleth: Yeah, so one of the really interesting things that I learned when I started researching this is that questions about the true sex or true gender of women in the Olympics happened immediately.

In 1928 it was the first year that women are allowed to run track at the Olympics. They had been allowed in other events before that that were deemed more feminine–so, like, swimming and tennis–but track and field, absolutely not until 1928. And immediately you hear the press, you hear sports officials saying, "There's something wrong with these women."

Feltman: It sounds like at that time it was more like, "Is it inherently unwomaning to be in sports?" [Laughs]

Eveleth: I mean, they genuinely believed that these women could turn themselves into men if they competed too much in athletics, like, that was an actual thing that they believed.

Feltman: Wow.

Eveleth: Now we have this ... very problematic idea around, like, a very rigid sex binary, right? That there's, like, XX, XY, like, you know, biological male, biological female ...

Feltman: Sure.

Eveleth: ... which obviously is not actually how humans are [laughs], you know, distributed–in this clear bimodal situation–but at the time they did not have that, right? At the time there was not this very clear sense of a very rigid sex binary. At the time the dominant idea–at least in the West: sort of Europe and the United States–was this idea called balance theory ...

Feltman: Hmm.

Eveleth: ... which was that every person was born with a certain amount of, like, male and female stuff inside of them and you could be, like, a 65 percent woman or a 99 percent woman, and that if you did certain things, that balance could shift.

So you could actually turn yourself into a man if you did manly things like participate in sports, especially if you were already kind of, like, a cuspy woman, you know [laughs], which

I feel like is actually, weirdly enough, maybe closer to reality in terms of, like, the spectrum of sex characteristics that exist ...

Feltman: Yeah.

Eveleth: But is not also correct [laughs].

Feltman: Right, right. It's still, it's still wrong, but it's–I'd love to, like, kind of go back to that drawing board and pick up a little bit of what they were putting down.

Yeah, you know, when you hear politicians today be like, "We used to know there were only two sexes; you know, now people are so confused," it's like, "Actually, listen, it's always been confusing, man." [laughs]

Eveleth: The whole time, yeah. Yeah, being a human, I think, is just inherently confusing in so many ways ...

Feltman: Yeah [laughs].

Eveleth: [Laughs] But, yeah, they really thought that these women were either really borderline cases, is what they would often say, or potentially gonna turn themselves into men, and so they decided that there needed to be rules and regulations to kind of test and check. And it all comes from a very paternalistic sense of like, "We need to protect these women from themselves because clearly no true woman would want to compete in athletics. That's, like, sort of not correct in some way."

Feltman: So how did that shift over time?

Eveleth: Yeah, so 1928 you immediately get people being like, "That's not a woman. That's not a woman." [Laughs] You know, like, you hear people talk about Hitomi Kinue, who is a Japanese runner, and in the newspapers they say, you know, "She has all the power of a halfback. She should be playing for the Chicago Bears," is a thing that they actually printed about this woman–which is also very funny, looking at it now, 'cause you, you know, you see photographs of these women, who are being described as, like, absolute units, and they just look like regular people ...

Feltman: Right.

Eveleth: Like, we look at athletes today, right, they're, like, incredibly jacked ...

Feltman: Right, but ...

Eveleth: Like, it's 1928 ...

Feltman: Because they're not actively fainting, they're [laughs] ...

Eveleth: [Laughs] Right, exactly. And so it's so funny just, like, how that line has shifted, but in 1936 the first official policy in that regard is passed by the International Amateur Athletic Federation [IAAF], which is now known as World Athletics, the governing body of track and field. And that policy allows them to pull aside any suspicious female, and they don't really say what warrants suspicion–it's sort of a very, like, "you'll know it when you see it" kind of situation. And the policy allows for an examination of that athlete, so that would be a nude inspection.

Feltman: Wow.

Eveleth: There are some intervening years where you have instructions like, "We really want you to go to your doctor and get examined and bring a little, like, note–like a doctor's note that says, like, 'diagnosed female,'" or whatever [laughs], you know?

Feltman: Yikes, wow.

Eveleth: Yeah, and then in 1966 they decide that doing this on a case-by-case basis, or sort of this ad hoc kind of way, is not good; we need to do it to all women. And they institute what are now known as the "nude parades," also sometimes known as the "peek and poke" tests, which were: every woman who competed in track and field had to go into a room and get naked in front of a panel—sometimes one person, sometimes more than one—to be confirmed that their body looked correct for a woman.

Feltman: Wow, gosh.

Eveleth: In 1968 they switch, and they change the policy, and they go to a chromosome test. And from 1968 to 1999, which is a very long period of time, every single woman who competed in the Olympics had to take a sex test, a chromosome-based sex test, and get a certificate of femininity that looks a little bit like your driver's license and bring it with you—everywhere you go, whenever you compete. And that lasts until 1999.

And the thing that's really interesting about this period of time is that immediately—like, as soon as the IOC [International Olympic Committee] and the IAAF start using these tests—you have doctors and scientists being like, "Whoa, whoa, whoa, hold on—this won't do any of the things that you say it's going to do. It will not necessarily catch all men who try to enter a women's competition because some men can have XX chromosomes. All you're going to do is catch women who have no idea there's anything different about them, who have shown up to the Olympics, trained their whole lives to compete and all of a sudden are gonna be told, 'Actually, surprise, you're not a woman, and you need to leave.'"

You know, there was a 30-year campaign by these scientists to write to the IOC, to write to World Athletics and be like, "Guys, like, don't do this. This doesn't work. It's not scientifically sound." The guy whose test they were using wrote to the IOC and the IAAF, being like, "Please stop doing this," and they were like, "No thanks," [laughs] you know?

When asked about it they basically say, like, "Look, I understand that you scientists in your labs have this way of thinking about things, but this is sports, and we do things our own way here."

And that was really, basically, the answer for 30 years, and it took a ton of work to try and convince these organizations to drop these tests.

Feltman: I can just kind of imagine someone being like, "Well, you didn't like it when we poked them and made them get naked. What do you want?" It's like, "It's very clear what we want; we want ..."

Eveleth: Just maybe don't–yeah.

Feltman: But okay–yeah, just don't.

And just to contextualize for listeners who might not be familiar with this topic, what are we talking about when we talk about intersex conditions, and how common are those variations?

Eveleth: Intersex is largely an identity, right, like queer that someone kind of opts into, that they say, like, "Yes, I am a part of this."

Feltman: Right.

Eveleth: There is the more medicalizing "differences of sex development," or DSD. A lot of intersex folks don't like that term because it is medicalizing, and they sort of say, like, "Well, there's actually nothing wrong with me; I'm just, you know–there's just this variation."

I tend to use sort of maybe a clunkier phrase of just, like, "people with sex variation," or, like, "people with variations in their sex biology."

It's also really hard to know how common this is because it sort of depends on how you define it. And also, in a lot of parts of the world, this is not documented; people aren't putting this into charts and stuff like that. So some experts estimate that the frequency, sort of broadly defined, of sex variations in the population is between one and two percent. So it's more common than identical twins.... It's not this incredibly rare thing that, like, only happens in these, like, super outlier situations.

Feltman: So do we have any sense of how many people were impacted by this?

Eveleth: We don't know how many women showed up to the Olympics or to the world championships or to, you know, a world athletics event, given this test and were told, "You need to leave."

The Olympics and the IAAF both were quite secretive about it in the sense that they did not share numbers, they did not share names–and, you know, in some ways you want that, right? You don't want to be outing people against their will about their biology.

The problem is that if you are an elite athlete, and you show up to a competition, you know pretty much everyone you're gonna be competing against, right? At this point you've been competing against them for years, probably. And so if someone shows up to the Olympics and then all of a sudden, like, doesn't compete, it's actually quite obvious, like, "Well, wait, what happened?"

And so they often were told to fake an injury. And they would, like, put a cast on somebody and have them, like, pretend to be injured. So we really don't know. I've heard a lot of different estimates. We're not talking about thousands of people here, right? You know, I've seen people estimate that something like a handful every Olympics between 1966 and 1988. And we also don't know how many people decided to stop showing up, right?

And so there were women who were terrified they were gonna fail these tests. We talked to one of them who actually paid for her own test before she went because she was so afraid she was gonna fail it. You know, she's heard all her life that, like, "Mm, you're maybe kind of a boy." And, like, she was like, "Well, I don't know–maybe I am. Like, I have no idea."

And so I think that's the other thing–is, like, we know that a handful every Olympics were sent home, but we don't know how many people sort of opted out entirely.

Feltman: So what's the situation today? You know, for the 2024 Olympics, how are they factoring this stuff in? I would love to assume they're not; I feel like that's probably not the case [laughs].

Eveleth: No, unfortunately. The International Olympic Committee, the IOC, they have said that there should not be policies that restrict people's participation based on their sex biology.

Feltman: Mm-hmm.

Eveleth: But they are actually not in charge of those policies; the different federations are. So you have: World Aquatics is the swimming one. World Athletics is the track-and-field one, right? Every sport has its own federation. And they're actually the ones who decide the rules of the sport and who gets to compete.

And different federations have different takes on this. Many federations just let people compete, right? But some don't. World Athletics, for example, does have a policy on the books—what they call DSD eligibility policies. And the situation today is that if you are an athlete who has one of their defined DSD conditions—so they have a list of which ones count, and essentially it's ones that offer you a high level of testosterone that your body can use—if you have one of these regulated ... DSDs, that means that you do have to manipulate your body's biology in order to lower your testosterone level down to a certain point: 2.5 nanomoles per liter.

There are two main ways you would do that. One of them is surgery. Some folks have internal gonads that produce high levels of testosterone, so you'd have to do surgery to remove those. That requires, basically, being on hormone replacement therapy for the rest of your life. It's obviously a permanent change.

The other option is to take medications to lower that testosterone level, and that's generally a combination of sort of an estrogen and an inhibitor drug that blocks testosterone. These are drugs that are often provided as gender-affirming care to trans youth to kind of stop puberty. They are not intended to lower [the testosterone level of] an adult woman who has a DSDs testosterone level. We don't actually have a great sense of what the side effects are gonna be for some of these people. It's sort of a big experiment because the World Medical Association, for example, has come out saying, like, "This is medically unethical. You should not be requiring people to take drugs to manipulate their biology so that they can compete in the sex category that they already occupy."

But because these federations are essentially independent bodies based internationally, there's not a lot of accountability. There was a case at the Court of Arbitration for Sport about this that Caster Semenya ruled on in 2019. And they agreed with the World Athletics. They said, "No, actually, it's okay for you to have these policies." So currently there are women who would love to be in Paris but are not because they can't compete unless they manipulate their bodies in this way.

Some of them have opted to try it. None of them were able to get their levels down and get their training back into place in time for Paris for this year. And some of them are saying, "No, I'm not gonna do that." I mean, it's expensive. Often these women are international, and they don't have a lot of resources. They don't have a doctor to prescribe this to them. They don't even know what drugs would be required. It's a lot of stuff to go through.

So that's where we're at currently. We are not gonna see a couple of athletes who, for example, were in the final in Tokyo last Olympics.

Feltman: If you wanna hear more about the history of sex testing in sports and how it's impacting the 2024 Olympics in Paris, check out Tested wherever you listen to your podcasts.

Science Quickly will be back on Friday with Episode Two of our ongoing Friday Fascination miniseries. This one is all about extreme archaeology, and if you missed the first episode you can go right on back and listen to it now.

Science Quickly is produced by me, Rachel Feltman, along with Fonda Mwangi, Kelso Harper, Madison Goldberg and Jeff DelViscio. Shayna Posses and Aaron Shattuck fact-check our show. Our theme music was composed by Dominic Smith. Subscribe to *Scientific American* for more up-to-date and in-depth science news.

For *Scientific American*, this is Rachel Feltman. See you next time.

About the Authors

Rachel Feltman is former executive editor of Popular Science *and forever host of the podcast* The Weirdest Thing I Learned This Week. *She previously founded the blog Speaking of Science for the* Washington Post.

Fonda Mwangi is an award-winning multimedia editor at Scientific American *and producer of* Science Quickly. *She previously worked at* Axios, *the* Recount *and* WTOP News. *She holds a master's degree in journalism and public affairs from American University in Washington, D.C.*

Jeffery DelViscio is currently chief multimedia editor/executive producer at Scientific American. *He is former director of multimedia at* STAT, *where he oversaw all visual, audio and interactive journalism. Before that he spent more than eight years at the* New York Times, *where he worked on five different desks across the paper. He holds dual master's degrees in journalism and in Earth and environmental sciences from Columbia University. He has worked onboard oceanographic research vessels and tracked money and politics in science from Washington, D.C. He was a Knight Science Journalism Fellow at the Massachusetts Institute of Technology in 2018. His work has won numerous awards, including two News and Documentary Emmy Awards.*

Section 4: Legislation and Violence

How Junk Science Is Being Used against Trans Kids

By Tulika Bose

Announcer 1: It is the latest fight over transgender rights.

Announcer 2: Arkansas passing a bill blocking gender affirming care for trans youth.

Announcer 3: Transgender kids in Texas are facing new barriers to accessing health care.

Tulika Bose: Right now you're probably seeing the fight for gender affirming care for trans kids play out across the country in your news feeds and all over the Internet.

Announcer 4: In 2022 the power of science and literature crumble in the face of the trans lobby.

Jules Gill-Peterson: We're seeing just sustained kind of moral panic and attack on the very idea of trans people, and so obviously science is being weaponized.

Announcer 4: One point biologists were allowed to determine what biology was, and there were two: male and female.

Bose: But there's one thing that keeps popping up over and over and over again in an attempt to discredit the rights of trans people: junk science. But first, what makes junk science, well, junk?

First, you have to understand the role that science has historically played in understanding sex and gender and how that's being weaponized today.

Announcer 4: You can't respond, "Oh, so men can become women" just by wishing it so. Tell us how that works.

Bose: I talked to Jules Gill-Peterson, a science historian and professor at Johns Hopkins, who studied the history of trans children, about the actual history of research that's attempted to define sex and gender.

Gill-Peterson: For a long time, the kind of research on, you know, gender, sex and trans people was incredibly poorly executed. And it was often done with outright prejudice. It was often done with very poor methodology. And it was often done in order to kind of increase social control of people, to force them to conform to a gender binary.

Bose: Let's rewind back to the 1940s and 1950s and specifically to the history of the word "gender."

Gill-Peterson: The crisis for both physicians and psychologists in the 1950s was that they had no idea what made people male or female. It wasn't chromosomes. It wasn't gonads, right? It wasn't hormonal composition. It wasn't genetics.

They couldn't find any one facet of biology that predicted reliably, right, who would be male or female. And then they were encountering all these people whose bodies didn't match how they felt on the inside.

As I had found when I was reading the medical records, they would assign intersex children a sex, right, and they would enforce surgeries and hormones on them to achieve that sex. But then the child wouldn't identify with that sex. And it would cause so much hardship. And so gender was sort of created just to make a conceptual distinction.

Bose: Peterson says the war against trans people actually has a basis in the same tenets that enforce scientific racism historically.

Gill-Peterson: We can talk about a kind of history of scientific racism that lots of people are familiar with that was basically sort of projecting social hierarchies, right, out into the world.

White, northern European scientists just kept discovering that they were apparently the superior race, right?

And you see this sort of shift, after World War II, away from kinds of biological explanations around race towards sort of cultural explanations that still come to the same conclusions.

Interestingly enough, the history of gender in medicine and psychology is actually a really key part of that.

Bose: And the thing is: a lot of outdated misinformation about sex, gender and trans people is still cited today.

Gill-Peterson: But I think sometimes that a line between junk science and legitimate science changes over time. So it's really easy for people to kind of cherry-pick ideas that they might want to use sort of out of context. And that's a lot of pressure to put on, you know, someone reading a newspaper article or scrolling Twitter.

Bose: And if you wanna talk about cherry-picking data, the very same psychologist who tried to enforce biological definitions of sex on kids were the same psychologists who accidentally discovered something else.

Gill-Peterson: Just that the idea that gender is separate from sex, as in separate from the body, that they don't always go together.

That's a concept that we often take for granted as being either associated with or invented by trans people somehow. It was an invention of behavioral psychologists who were working very closely with researchers in endocrinology in the 1940s and 1950s.

But they couldn't force children to then identify as boys or girls. That was their big problem. The team talk about this in a series of papers in 1955, published at Hopkins. They say gender is basically just your sense of being a boy or a girl.

Bose: And science has come a long way. It's increasingly understood now that gender isn't a binary.

Peterson says there's still a lot of misconceptions masquerading as scientific consensus.

Gill-Peterson: The biggest, right, is that there is scientific consensus on what makes people male or female or what makes people trans. The anti-trans side invokes really outdated scientific concepts.

The idea that "Oh, we know what makes people male or female. It's either genitals or our idea of chromosomes."

Anyone worth their salt will tell you XX and XY are not the only chromosomal combinations for humans.

Bose: So how and why should we debunk junk science?

Gill-Peterson: Before I even decide if I would want to debunk something, I first just wanna contextualize: "Where did this data come from?"

Their work may have been passed peer review 20 or 30 years ago, but it wouldn't today.

Bose: And we don't need to go far to see moral panic. A 2018 study by a Brown University researcher suggesting that peer pressure could make kids trans led a journal to republish a corrected version. But that same study is being used against trans kids right now.

Gill-Peterson: So I think actually the tools that we would bring, right, say to debunking race science or other kinds of just extremely unscientific but also extremely objectionable weaponizations of scientific discourse, I think we can use those same principles. So if we start from a point of view where we're unafraid to say, like, "Look, I don't like junk science directed at trans people, because it harms trans people, and it's bad science," right?

RFK, Jr., Releases Report Attacking Medical Care for Trans Children

By Dan Vergano

On Wednesday Secretary of Health and Human Services Robert F. Kennedy, Jr., released a study that is critical of gender-affirming care for minors. It updates a widely criticized study that was released in May.

The American Medical Association and numerous other major medical organizations support psychological and medical treatments that help transgender children live as the gender they identify as. Between 2.5 and 8.4 percent of children identify as transgender or gender-diverse. This means they identify with a different gender than, or have a gender expression that does not conform to, the norms of their sex assigned at birth. Gender-affirming treatment can include puberty-blocking hormones and sex hormones such as testosterone and estrogen. The effects of puberty blockers are reversible; sex hormones cause more lasting effects.

The newly-published Department of Health and Human Services report claims that gender-affirming care is harmful–in contrast with widespread medical consensus. An HHS press release asserts that it found that "the harms from sex-rejecting procedures–including puberty blockers, cross-sex hormones, and surgical operations–are significant, long term, and too often ignored or inadequately tracked." In a statement in that press release, RFK, Jr., said that such care has "inflicted lasting physical and psychological damage on vulnerable young people."

The earlier May report from HHS attracted criticism for a lack of transparency about who its authors were and for its advocacy of unproven psychotherapy for transgender and gender-diverse kids, a population at high risk of suicide. The new report revealed its nine authors, most of whom are known critics of gender-affirming care.

"Now that the authors have announced themselves, they can be identified as engineers of a cottage industry that solely exists to dismantle health care for a vulnerable group of people," says Meredithe McNamara, an adolescent medicine specialist at the Yale School of Medicine and a co-author of an influential critique of the U.K.'s 2024 Cass Review of gender-affirming care. "Transgender identity is real, transgender people of all ages thrive when they have access to the care they need, and politics needs to get out of medicine."

"Calling this report 'political' is simply wrong," says HHS press secretary Emily Hilliard. "We will continue to follow the science wherever it leads, even when the findings challenge entrenched interests or preferred narratives."

"Our group included clinicians and researchers from across the political spectrum. We were given full independence by the administration to follow the evidence wherever it led," said HHS study co-author Evgenia Abbruzzese, in a statement sent by a representative. She adds that the reassessment of gender-affirming care "reflects a familiar medical pattern: well-intentioned innovation followed by evidence-based correction."

An HHS news release included peer reviews of the new report, including one from the American Psychiatric Association (APA), which found that "its underlying methodology lacks sufficient transparency and clarity for its findings to be taken at face value." The report authors rejected the criticism. (The APA says its stands by its critique.) The American Academy of Pediatrics and the Endocrine Society declined to review the report, according to a statement in the report.

"Gender-affirming care is not fringe; it's standard, developmentally appropriate health care," says pediatrician Bianca Allison, a fellow with Physicians for Reproductive Health, in response to the HHS report. "It is individualized, careful and–as every major medical organization has stated and a mounting body of evidence indicates–can be lifesaving."

The new report's release follows Republican political campaigns over the past several years that have focused on restricting trans kids' participation in sports and use of locker rooms in schools. President Donald Trump issued a January executive order entitled "Protecting Children from Chemical and Surgical Mutilation." The executive order has contributed to widespread closures of hospital programs treating transgender and gender-diverse kids following threats of federal funding being withdrawn.

The AMA and AAP later released a joint statement on Wednesday, to "reject characterizations of our approach to gender-affirming care as negligent or ideologically driven, and take particular issue with the false assertion that our members have committed 'malpractice' or betrayed their oath in any way. These claims, rooted in politics and partisanship, misrepresent the consensus of medical science, undermine the professionalism of physicians, and risk harming vulnerable young people and their families."

About the Author

Dan Vergano is senior editor, Washington, D.C., at Scientific American. *He has previously written for Grid News, BuzzFeed News,* National Geographic *and* USA Today. *He is chair of the New Horizons committee for the Council for the Advancement of Science Writing and a journalism award judge for both the American Association for the Advancement of Science and the U.S. National Academies of Sciences, Engineering, and Medicine.*

Laws Vilifying Transgender Children and Their Families Are Abusive

By Tey Meadow & Kristina R. Olson

On Monday, it became illegal to talk about gender identity or sexual orientation in hundreds of classrooms throughout the state of Florida. This law is one of historic numbers of proposed laws and measures targeting trans youth in Texas, Arizona, Alabama, and more than one dozen other U.S. states. Tens of thousands of transgender children and teenagers currently live in states where lawmakers seek to exclude them from playing sports, eliminate mention of people like them in schools, or criminalize transgender-affirming medical care, and the introduction of these measures come despite growing social approval of transgender Americans.

We are social scientists who have studied transgender youth and their families for more than a decade. Social acceptance and affirmative support are the keys to mental health for transgender children. The prospective laws and policies propose the very opposite: encouraging the mistreatment of trans youth and inciting fear in compassionate adults.

In a desperate attempt to stop these damaging measures, children and families do what they must: out themselves to major media outlets despite the risks of prosecution, stand as plaintiffs in legal efforts to stop these laws, and share deeply personal traumas and intimate health histories on traditional and social media platforms.

In Idaho, where lawmakers debated a law making it a felony to provide trans-affirmative medical care, a trans teenager testified that the idea of going through puberty made her contemplate suicide. In Kentucky, a 12-year-old described her sadness at learning she could not join a field hockey team because she is transgender.

When the governor and attorney general of Texas recently directed the state's Department of Family and Protective Services to investigate parents who provide teenagers with gender-affirmative medical care, a parent targeted by one of those investigations described the terror she and her child experienced at the idea they might be separated.

While purporting to protect these kids or their cisgender peers from abuse, these hearings are themselves abusive—and inappropriate. In Missouri, while testifying against a proposed anti-trans sports bill, a Republican senator asked a 14-year-old trans girl if she was "gonna go through the procedure?"—meaning this politician asked a child in a public forum whether she was going to have genital surgery.

These laws don't merely compel vulnerable people to perform their terror and vulnerability for audiences of lawmakers, media and judges in hopes of reversing, vetoing or voting down these efforts. They force petrified children and families to lobby for human dignity. Even when the bills fail, or, in the case of Texas or Arkansas, a court prevents the laws or decrees from being enforced, they cause harm—by reinforcing the misguided notion that trans people are troubled and by signaling to trans children and their families that they are not welcome in their states or communities.

Trans youth who receive support from their families, peers and communities have similar levels of self-esteem and are not more depressed than youth who are not transgender. Perhaps the most surprising finding from our research is just how unsurprising the lives of trans youth can be, when they feel safe in their families and communities. It is when they lack support from their parents, lack access to appropriate facilities—such as bathrooms and medical care—and when they fear for their emotional, material and bodily safety that trans youth suffer.

Despite the near-consensus among experts on the negative impact of these laws, some politicians are mobilizing anti-transgender bias to gain favor with voters. The Texas decree came mere days before the state's primary elections. Tennessee's law banned medical transition for prepubescent children, even though literally no transgender medicine takes place before puberty. Governor Jim Justice of West Virginia signed a law banning transgender children from participating in sports, and then acknowledged that he was unable to identify a single instance of a transgender child gaining advantage in any competitive sport in the state.

So, why put these laws in place? Since political orientation is strongly correlated with perspective on trans acceptance, trans youth have become an expedient vehicle for showcasing one's conservatism. This is most evident when you consider that that these mandates and proposed bills contravene the advice of every major medical, psychiatric and pediatric organization in the United States.

Trans kids testify at legislative hearings, because they fear they have no alternative. They have little interest in inviting reporters into their living rooms to discuss the latest tweet from a politician, and they certainly don't want to read yet another story in the media about their own suffering. But they do these things to help themselves and their peers.

Our view is that trans youth should not need to publicly share their suicidal thoughts, discuss their genitalia with politicians, or develop emergency plans should they be taken away from their families, but rather should be given the same dignity that other children are provided. And adults should not need them to demonstrate their suffering in order to provide them with the same basic rights to health and happiness as their peers.

Some people are beginning to hear this message. Governor Spencer Cox of Utah vetoed his state's efforts to outlaw trans girls' participation in girls' sports. In so doing, he likely placed himself at a political disadvantage; he's a Republican, with a conservative base, and the Utah legislature eventually overrode his veto. Cox recognized the humanity of the trans kids in his state, writing in an official letter to legislative leaders: "I don't understand what they are going through or why they feel the way they do. But I want them to live. And all the research shows that even a little acceptance and connection can reduce suicidality significantly." Noting that there were just four transgender kids playing high school sports in Utah, Cox wrote that he hoped "we can work to find ways to show these four kids that we love them and they have a place in our state." We hope that leaders of every party in every state will one day send that message to trans kids, too.

About the Authors

Tey Meadow is an associate professor of sociology at Columbia University and author of Trans Kids: Being Gendered in the Twenty-First Century.

Kristina R. Olson is a professor of psychology at Princeton University, where she directs the Human Diversity Lab and the Trans Youth Project.

How Anti-LGBTQ+ Rhetoric Fuels Violence

By Helen Santoro

The FBI recently arrested a man who had threatened to kill a doctor in Boston who provides gender-affirming care to transgender children. The following day, members of two far-right groups, the Patriot Front and the Proud Boys, gathered outside of a Unitarian church in Columbus, Ohio, leading to the cancellation of a drag queen story hour. These incidents came just weeks after a mass shooting at Club Q, an LGBTQ+ club in Colorado Springs, which was planning to host a drag performance to honor the upcoming Transgender Day of Remembrance.

Such attacks are part of a staggering rise in anti-LGBTQ+ violence and threats across the country. While the motives of these events are not always clear, as of 2020, around one out of every five hate crimes committed in the U.S. were motivated by anti-LGBTQ+ bias, according to the U.S. Department of Justice.

The fuel for much of this violence has been far-right rhetoric spread by white nationalist groups, extremist influencers and conservative politicians, says Yotam Ophir, an assistant professor of communications at the University at Buffalo, who studies misinformation and extremism. "It's become pretty clear that the LGBTQ+ community is now at the heart of the new iteration of the culture wars that we have been unfortunately going through in recent years," he says. This community has become "a staple of right-wing messaging and often propaganda."

Part of the reason this rhetoric is so prominent now is because of connections with evangelical Christian and white nationalist movements, says Sophie Bjork-James, an assistant professor of anthropology at Vanderbilt University and an expert in white nationalism and the religious right. According to Bjork-James, both movements are based around the patriarchy, which requires two genders that are in a hierarchical relationship with each other. "Queer identities challenge the patriarchy," she says.

During the 2016 presidential election, white nationalists and evangelicals supported then candidate Donald Trump, bringing extremist views that were once on the periphery of mainstream politics to the center of the Republican Party, Bjork-James says. There is also a growing fear among conservatives, Ophir says, that the U.S. is becoming less white and less Christian. All of these factors have fueled the rise of far-right media personalities such as Chaya Raichik, who runs the social media account Libs of TikTok, political commentator Matt Walsh and Fox News host Tucker Carlson.

"The way that [far-right media instigators] tend to work is that they have an audience whom they have already primed for violence and for hate," says Erin Reed, a legislative researcher, content creator and trans rights activist. They will then target a specific person or organization and blast misinformation out to their millions of follows, she says.

For example, earlier this year, Raichik, Walsh and Carlson all spread a baseless conspiracy theory that Boston Children's Hospital's gender-affirming health care clinic was performing hysterectomies (removals of the uterus) on children. Afterward, the hospital received multiple bomb threats. The reality is that the clinic requires patients to be at least 18 years old to perform a gender-affirming hysterectomy. Additionally, data from more than a dozen studies clearly show that access to gender-affirming care–much of which is nonsurgical–is linked to better mental health outcomes in trans kids and that lack of access to such care is associated with higher rates of suicidal thoughts, depression and self-harming behavior.

Scientific American reached out to Raichik, Walsh and Carlson for comment, but none responded to the questions presented.

The false claims and rhetoric used by right-wing extremists dehumanize and vilify the LGBTQ+ community and provoke stochastic terrorism, a phenomenon in which hate speech increases the likelihood that people will attack the targets of vicious claims.

Research has also shown that this type of rhetoric can motivate people to express and possibly act on their prejudiced views.

The potential for any individual extremist message to push people toward violence is low, Ophir says. But continuous exposure to this hate speech from many different media platforms and politicians can contribute to radicalization.

The rise in anti-LGBTQ+ hate messaging has also emboldened conservative lawmakers. For example, Tennessee legislators who sponsored a bill that seeks to ban gender-affirming care for trans youth said that they based the proposed legislation in part around Walsh's social media crusade against Vanderbilt University Medical Center, which provides gender-affirming care. Walsh also helped stage a rally in support of this bill in October, which was attended by GOP members, including Republican Senator Marsha Blackburn of Tennessee and that state's Senate Majority Leader Jack Johnson.

A number of Republican politicians strongly embraced anti-LGBTQ+ rhetoric during the recent midterm elections. Illinois's Republican nominee for governor referred to gender-affirming care for trans youth as "experimental gender surgeries," which is not accurate because such surgeries have been shown to be safe, and patients have very low rates of regret. Another GOP politician–a candidate for attorney general in Nevada–called for there to be "a lot less" trans people. In the final weeks leading up to the elections, extremist candidates and groups such as America First Legal–an ultraconservative legal organization run by former Trump adviser Stephen Miller–poured around $50 million dollars into anti-trans ads, many of which targeted parents and spread misinformation about gender-affirming care. Such hate speech from politicians boosts the likelihood of domestic terrorism, according to a 2020 study led by a researcher at Pennsylvania State University.

"Antiqueer rhetoric seeks to establish violence against the LGBTQ+ community, be it physical violence, harassment and abuse, or political violence," Reed says.

Combating hate speech is difficult but not impossible, Bjork-James says. Supporting LGBTQ+ people who have been targeted online by sharing their stories is a good first step. Additionally, people can fight back against misinformation by reporting social media accounts that are spreading anti-LGBTQ+ rhetoric and putting pressure on advertisers who support platforms with hate speech, she adds. More Internet regulation would help—something that has become particularly relevant since billionaire Elon Musk bought Twitter and reinstated many far-right accounts, Ophir says.

Additionally, education on how to navigate the media and Internet is vitally important. "As humans, we're not wired to cope with so much information," he says. "We should provide people with better tools to understand how media works, to understand how to identify falsehoods and to identify propaganda."

Unfortunately, it's unlikely we have seen the worst of the anti-LGBTQ+ violence in the U.S., Reed says. But many states are fighting back through legislation that protects LGBTQ+ people, she notes. California, for example, just became the first sanctuary state for transgender youth who are seeking gender-affirming care. Washington, D.C., also passed legislation that protects the rights of those pursuing care for abortion and gender affirmation.

We must remember that we have the power to advocate for LGBTQ+ rights and make a difference, Ophir says. "I think this is our biggest failure as humans: our inability to imagine change," he says. "We need to keep fighting back."

About the Author

Helen Santoro is a science journalist who writes about health, medicine and LGBTQ+ communities.

Families Find Ways to Protect Their LGBTQ Kids

By Marla Broadfoot

Tamara had not been sleeping well. Some days she woke up at four o'clock in the morning in tears and overwhelmed by a feeling of helplessness. She had moved her family three times over the past six years. Her house in New Hampshire was shot at—possibly by someone aiming at the rainbow signs in her front yard. In 2022 she fled to Massachusetts, which seemed to be safer for her child, Grey, who is transgender. But whenever she hears the words "safe state," a thought pops into her head: "Austria felt like a safe place in World War II, too."

For the time being, Grey feels like they are in a good place mentally. (For their personal safety, the names of young people and their parents in this story have been changed.) They have found a community that sees them for who they are and a state that allows them to receive the gender-affirming care they need. But they have seen dark times before, and the familiar drumbeat of anxiety never quite goes away. "I am always a little concerned in the back of my head that things are getting kind of bad in some places, and maybe that'll happen to me," Grey says.

For many families with LGBTQ kids, the dark times are now. More than 500 anti-LGBTQ bills were considered in state legislatures in 2023, and 84 passed. (The term "LGBTQ" refers to lesbian, gay, and other people with minority sexual orientations and gender identities.) These bills restrict discussions of LGBTQ people or history in schools, limit legal protections for queer and transgender youth, and prohibit transgender health care for minors and even adults.

The sheer volume of these bills, and the sentiment behind them, is doing harm. An estimated 71 percent of LGBTQ youths—including 86 percent of transgender and nonbinary kids—say that laws concerning LGBTQ people have had a negative impact on their mental health. Nearly half of LGBTQ kids seriously considered suicide in the previous year, according to a survey conducted in 2022 by the Trevor Project, a nonprofit group that offers crisis services.

Discrimination against LGBTQ kids is also taking a toll on parents' mental health, and the added family stress can make things even worse for their children. Studies show that family support is critical to the psychological resilience of queer and trans kids. But many parents are filled with fear, grief and anxiety, and the strain makes it harder for them to shield their children from the harshness of an often hostile world. "No one can be empathic with your fists clenched," says Lisa Diamond, a psychologist at the University of Utah. "I've come to believe that we cannot help LGBTQ youth without taking stock of the amount of vigilance and worry that is eating up the nervous systems of their parents. You can't heal one without the other, because if that kid really matters to you, there is no way that their fear can't make you afraid."

In reporting this story, I spoke with 20 parents, and some of their kids, in North Carolina, Georgia, Texas, Florida, Ohio, California, New York and Massachusetts. Our conversations revealed just how widespread their fears are. Tamara, Grey's mom, tried for months to stop anti-LGBTQ bills when she lived in New Hampshire. She and others were spit at and called "groomers" and "pedophiles" after speaking at a legislative session. Then there were the bullets grazing her house.

Still, families are finding ways to cope. A grassroots movement is creating safe spaces for parents, such as online communities that enable parents and caregivers to support one another and networks to help them find LGBTQ-friendly places to raise their kids. They are crafting positive narratives, focused on their families, filled with strength and growth and hope. Those narratives are helping them make meaning from their hardship while envisioning a future where their loved ones are no longer under attack.

Francis came out to their family as pansexual and nonbinary in 10th grade, with a group text. The text explained that they would prefer to be called by a new name and referred to with they/them pronouns, and although they didn't expect their conservative Catholic family to understand, they hoped their relatives would respect their wishes.

"I was terrified," Francis recalls. They had been seeing a therapist for years, but the counselor wasn't well versed in LGBTQ issues. "I knew I needed to come out so that I could get further support, whether that be from another therapist or somebody in my family at least recognizing my pronouns and my name," Francis says.

The first texts Francis got back from family members were positive: "we love you for who you are." But within a few months they learned that their parents had quite different feelings. Their dad ignored the issue, staying silent rather than using Francis's new name and pronouns. Their mom, Lois, kept questioning what it meant for them to be nonbinary or trans. She knew people who were trans, "but when it is your own kid," she says, "it seems so different."

Given the large number of young people who identify as LGBTQ–about 25 percent of high school students are not heterosexual, according to a 2021 survey–remarkably little research has focused on the experiences of their parents, says David Huebner, a clinical psychologist at the George Washington University. The queer community has compensated for lost family ties with the narrative of a "chosen family": even if your parents reject you, you can depend on other LGBTQ people, who become like siblings. That sentiment might work for adults, but it doesn't ring true for minors who rely on their families for even the most basic needs.

In 2009 Huebner and Caitlin Ryan, director of the Family Acceptance Project at San Francisco State University, published one of the first studies showing that parents' attitudes matter a lot. The research found that lesbian, gay or bisexual teens who were rejected by their parents or caregivers were eight times more likely to attempt suicide than those who were accepted.

But parents' reactions don't necessarily fit into the simplistic binary of rejecting or accepting. "It's a journey, a very bumpy journey," says Roberto Abreu, a psychologist at the University of Florida. Abreu and others have shown that parents can experience a gamut of emotions after their kid comes out as queer or trans–shock, confusion, sadness, worry, guilt, fear, grief, anger–and it can take two years or more for those emotions to abate. They often feel overwhelmed by the disconnect between their earlier beliefs about their child's identity and what that child is telling them now. The burden of navigating schools, health care, and other systems to support their child adds to the strain.

"There's just a lot of stress and anxiety around the unknown; like, what am I supposed to do?" Lois says. She and her husband held wildly different views on gender and how to care for Francis, which caused a fracture in their marriage. "It's like walking on glass. It's really scary," she says.

Some parents grieve the loss of the child they thought they had and their visions for that child's future. These expectations are often tied to outdated conceptions of gender and sexual orientation that are being challenged as more people come out as LGBTQ and expand our understanding of human experience. For example, gender is not necessarily fixed at birth. A study in JAMA Network Open found that most transgender children sense a mismatch between their biological sex and their gender identity by age seven. Sarah, the mother of a six-year-old transgender girl in New York State, still feels a pang whenever she comes across something adorned with her daughter's male birth name, which many trans people call a deadname. She and her husband named each of their children after a relative who had passed away to keep the memory of their deceased loved ones alive.

"That's a complicated thing for parents, I think, because how can you feel grief over something that clearly your kid is experiencing joy over–being their true selves?" Sarah says. Sarah recalls reading somewhere that grief is just love with no place to go, and those words resonated with her.

Unresolved grieving for a person who is still present yet different is an experience that psychologists sometimes refer to as ambiguous loss. In families of LGBTQ children, such loss may affect not just the parents but also their kids. Work led by Jenifer McGuire, a professor of family social science at the University of Minnesota, suggests transgender children can experience ambiguous loss when their family responds to their identity in conflicting ways. Family members might remain physically present but become psychologically absent, ignoring the gender transition and prompting a sense of loss in the children.

For Francis, there was a certain amount of sadness when their expectations of what life would be like after coming out brushed up against reality. They transferred to a new high school, where they met some like-minded friends. Their mom got them into a gender clinic in Ohio, where they were referred to a psychologist who helped them address their distress at the mismatch between their gender identity and their sex assigned at birth. Psychiatrists, after thorough consultation, recommended they start their medical transition with hormone treatments. But during one appointment, Francis's dad said he thought what they were doing was wrong and insisted they forgo treatment.

"It was really earth-shattering," Francis says. "I had been very sad about a lot of things, about not being accepted by everybody. But when he had completely shut it down, I was very, very angry. We've gone through the other possibilities, we've gone through the other options, and all the doctors are telling you that this is what needs to happen."

Every major medical association in the U.S., including the American Academy of Pediatrics, the American Medical Association and the Endocrine Society, endorses gender-affirming care for trans kids. Such care ranges from counseling to social affirmation to medical interventions such as hormone therapy. Numerous research studies have linked this form of care to better mental health. For example, one study looked at nearly 22,000 trans people nationwide who sought hormone therapy. It found that those who started receiving hormones as teens had fewer suicidal thoughts and a lower rate of substance abuse than those who were forced to wait until adulthood.

Still, Francis was afraid to argue with their dad. Lois, their mom, promised she would never let their dad kick them out of the family home, but Francis wasn't so sure. "The scared part of me was [thinking]: Don't say too much. Because I still need a place to live. I still need a safe space."

Lois was angry and scared, too, and worried that Francis would lose hope. She reminded them that they would turn 18 in a little more than a year and suggested they make a calendar to count down the days.

Francis put the date into their phone, but seeing the time tick by in an interminable number of hours and minutes only fueled their anxiety. So they bought several packs of colorful Post-It notes, numbered each for the hundreds of days they had left until the birthday that would give them independence and pasted them all over one wall of their bedroom. "It was a bizarre thing to do," Francis says. But the notes kept them going.

Compared with other kids their age, LGBTQ youths are at higher risk of numerous mental health issues, including depression, anxiety, substance abuse, self-harm and suicide. These health issues have been largely ascribed to minority stress, the consequences of social sources of tension that come with a marginalized identity. These stressors are not an innate part of an LGBTQ identity. Rather they emerge from experiencing repeated prejudice and powerlessness.

Now some researchers believe that the minority stress theory should be expanded to include parents of queer and trans kids, who experience a loss of privilege and normalcy and contend with oppressive institutions on behalf of their family. In a small study of 40 parents of transgender children, parents reported experiencing rejection from their extended family, as relatives refused to learn about their children's transition or criticized their parenting. They feared being mistreated by friends, other parents and their community for not enforcing societal norms surrounding gender identity.

For many families, the moment a kid comes out of the closet, the parents get into the closet, unsure of how to deal with a secret that is not their own. When Cristina, a mother in North Carolina, first learned that her oldest kid was bisexual, she worried about how the members of her conservative church would react. "There was a lot of fear. I didn't want people to know; I didn't know how to frame it," she recalls. "I was just terrified that I was going to be cast out of my circles and not supported if I supported my kid. So I went underground with that info."

This type of anticipated rejection or stigma is a key driver of minority stress. Coming out is often considered a lifelong process because people who are queer or trans must constantly negotiate how openly they want to exist in society, deciding whether they should share that aspect of their identity or keep it to themselves. "One of the things that is associated with negative mental health outcomes for LGBTQ people is concealment. And concealment is basically the flip side of outness," says Josh Goodman, a psychologist at Southern Oregon University. "The same thing goes for parents, too."

Simon, a gay teen, recalls how as a child he would hide his dolls whenever guests visited. Although he expected his parents to be supportive, he says it was still hard to tell them he was gay, "like pulling a knife out of your throat." When he was in the seventh grade, he was at a neighborhood convenience store when a man called him a "disgusting f****t." Simon put down the drink he was about to buy and walked straight home. Every time he goes back to that store, which he does often, he feels a little sick to his stomach. "That moment is instilled in my mind."

His mom didn't learn about the episode until weeks later, and when she did, she was filled with guilt that she somehow had allowed it to happen. She decided to send Simon to a more progressive, accepting high school one county away. She started daring herself to tell people he was gay, as if educating those around him were a talisman against future harm. And she tried to follow his lead whenever possible. "If he's going to be fearless, I need to be fearless," she says.

Fear is a major source of stress for many parents of LGBTQ kids. They worry their kids will be lonely, suffer from poor mental health, and experience violence or victimization. And those worries cause parents to react in ways they are not always proud of. One mother told me she cried when her daughter came out to her as bisexual: "I just knew that her life was going to be so much more difficult."

This notion that being gay means pain and suffering reinforces stigma, yet it has some basis in reality. According to a 2023 study by the Trevor Project, 24 percent of LGBTQ youths reported that they were physically threatened or harmed in the past year because of either their sexual orientation or their gender identity; those who were threatened or harmed also reported attempting suicide at nearly triple the rate of those who were not.

Jacqueline, a mother of two in Florida, was roused from her sleep one September morning as the telephone persistently rang several rooms away. The mother of a friend of one of her children, Adrian, was on the line. She wanted to know if the youngster was okay. Adrian had texted suicide notes to that friend and others in the middle of the night. Jacqueline rushed out of her room and found Adrian lying on the floor, convulsing. On the ambulance ride to the hospital, her mind was a jumble of worry and dread.

"Is Adrian going to be okay? Is there going to be brain damage? I didn't know," Jacqueline recalls. "I was in shock. I thought, I can't believe this is happening; I just cannot believe this is happening."

Adrian had come out as trans to their parents the year before, when they were 14. Adrian's father, who came from a conservative background, consistently misgendered them. The boys at their school were all bigger and appeared more masculine, and they felt like their gender was constantly being questioned. Eventually it got to be too much, and Adrian sent those texts.

Five years later and after many hours spent under the care of medical professionals, Adrian is doing well. They're a junior in college, living in an apartment with their older brother 15 minutes away from their parents. Their father finally accepted their identity. Jacqueline texts them every day, and if they sound "off," she rushes over to see them. "I always worry," she says. "I'm still scared that something might happen."

Diamond, the University of Utah psychologist, says this hypervigilant state can be devastating to parents. She has studied minority stress in members of the LGBTQ community and in their caregivers, and she believes the absence of safety erodes their mental health. The same response designed to protect humans from the proverbial saber-toothed tiger is now perpetually activated by headlines signaling that LGBTQ kids are threatened.

"We humans need to feel a sense of belonging–it's our birthright as a social species," Diamond says. "When we feel that there's something about us or our family that's off, then we just go into that evolutionary state of watch out." Diamond's work suggests that being in that constant state of uncertainty could be as detrimental to a person's overall well-being as experiencing a traumatic event. Her research indicates that all this worry can cause some parents to become more controlling and authoritarian, driven by the desire to protect their kids from danger or judgment.

For example, parents might keep their kids from LGBTQ-centric events such as Pride parades or discourage them from publicly disclosing their pronouns. Even if the intention is to protect, these tactics can create a vicious cycle. One recent study linked higher levels of parental psychological control–that is, trying to coerce kids into thinking or behaving differently–with more depressive symptoms among LGBTQ youth.

Looking back, Tamara regrets how she insisted on constantly cutting Grey's hair and nails, nervous about what would happen if they didn't adhere to the gender norms of the rural Texas town where they first lived. Although Grey recalls being bitter about it at the time, they can see now why their mom thought their identity had to be kept under wraps. "You don't necessarily want to be the weird feminine one mixed in with that group of people," Grey says. "She wasn't really making a bad decision in my mind. It's hard to figure out what to do because both decisions are kind of hurtful, just in different ways."

In helping their kids embrace their authentic selves while trying to keep them out of harm's way, parents of LGBTQ youth are walking a tightrope between freedom and safety. That act is getting even trickier as anti-LGBTQ legislation sweeps the nation. "I think the burden of these bans, and stigma and discrimination more broadly, on the population is even bigger than we estimate," says Kerith Conron, research director at the Williams Institute, based at the University of California, Los Angeles, School of Law. "It's not just the individual; it's these broader ecological ripple effects."

Researchers working to understand the child-parent dynamic have been harassed by some of the same groups trying to make the lives of LGBTQ people and their families so miserable. Last year Abreu, the psychologist at the University of Florida, partnered with Russ Toomey, a developmental scientist at the University of Arizona, and the Human Rights Campaign (HRC) Foundation to conduct the first large-scale, national study of parents and caregivers of trans and nonbinary children. The study gathered parents' perspectives in a variety of contexts, asking about their mental health and their child's gender identity development, the barriers they faced and the support systems that helped them. The researchers shared the survey through the HRC Foundation and online groups where parents of trans youth congregate. More than 1,400 parents responded.

But anti-trans groups got ahold of the survey and sent hostile e-mails to Abreu and Toomey. One group penned letters to their universities' presidents and institutional review boards, as well as boards of regents, governors and heads of the departments of education in both states, claiming the research was unethical and was harming youth. "That's the first time I've ever had an outside entity file a grievance against the ethics of research that I have engaged in in nearly 20 years," Toomey says. "That professional attack is quite jarring to take."

Toomey is working on publishing the study results. He hopes the research will inform policies to better support and educate the parents of trans youth.

Unlike parents of children in many other minority groups, most of those raising queer and trans kids don't have lived experiences to inform them and are often unsure how to support their LGBTQ offspring. So they are turning to peer-support groups. PFLAG, formerly known as Parents, Families and Friends of Lesbians and Gays, runs such groups, and many parents have found a sense of purpose and belonging that has helped them strengthen relationships with their children. But some parents aren't comfortable talking about these issues in a group setting. Others live in communities without a local chapter; according to some estimates, only about 10 to 15 percent of parents of LGBTQ children ever make it to a PFLAG meeting.

Instead many parents gather virtually, seeking crowd-sourced advice from Reddit or joining one of countless Facebook groups. Every day these platforms are filled with posts from parents searching for information and a sense of community. They are looking for recommendations on affirming churches and therapists; asking for guidance on sex talks and same-sex sleepovers; talking through experiences with school bullies, haircuts and hormone therapies. These online communities can help parents navigate this journey, giving them a place to open up to other parents who have been in their position before and can show them what's ahead. More experienced parents can correct commonly held misconceptions and connect newcomers to resources that can help them better understand and support their kid.

One such online community, called Mama Bears, started in 2014 with 150 members, most of them conservative Christians. Cristina, the mom in North Carolina, was one of them. She says the group supported her as she reexamined her faith, a process that was often frightening and messy. "[We were] holding each other up but at the same time challenging each other to continue movingforward," she says, "to start learning about what acceptance of your kid really means."

Today Mama Bears is more wide-ranging, with more than 39,000 members and various programs serving the greater LGBTQ community. Liz Dyer, the group's founder, says she has seen a complete shift in the conversations parents are having, moving from topics such as religious acceptance to concerns about protecting their children. "Mothers are very worried. But what we have found is that knowledge and education really empower parents. And once they feel more empowered and capable and knowledgeable, a lot of their anxiety–I don't want to say it dissipates, but it's easier for them to cope with."

In addition to the communities parents are building for themselves, some LGBTQ-focused organizations are expanding their services to help families. In Austin, Tex., a small nonprofit called Out Youth has created several programs for parents, including "family office hours" that offer hour-long counseling sessions for caregivers and family members. It also started caregiver-support groups, which provide a six-week crash course on parenting a trans, nonbinary or questioning child. And Out Youth piloted a caregiver peer-support program, which paired more experienced parents of trans kids with those whose kids had just come out.

"The thing that I've learned, and that I've said from the beginning of doing this work, is that caregivers and their young person are on separate yet intersecting journeys," says Sarah Kapostasy, who formerly served as Out Youth's clinical director. "Sometimes caregivers need a separate space." If parents have a place where they can figure things out away from their family, it can keep their kids from being burdened by negative feelings those parents are going through and from taking on such feelings about themselves.

Eventually many parents experience a kind of positive transformation as they adjust to their child's identity, research suggests, and they often end up redefining their own identity as the parent of an LGBTQ kid. Dani Rosenkrantz, a psychologist and researcher in Florida, says that although parenting a trans kid is often cast as a hard role filled with grief and pain, she has heard a more positive narrative emerge lately about parents witnessing their worldviews expand and their children flourish.

"I have learned so much from my child, and I just feel very proud of who she is and how she's had the courage to speak that truth," Sarah, the mother in New York, told me. "We owe it to our kids to make a more informed, enlightened world for them." One study by researchers at the University of Kentucky set out to catalog the positive aspects of parenting an LGBTQ child. The survey of 142 parents uncovered various ways the experience brought about parents' personal growth. It made them more compassionate, gave them greater empathy for marginalized populations, strengthened their relationship with their children, connected them more fully to their values, led to lasting friendships, and motivated them to engage in activism and advocacy.

But trying to make the world a better place for their own kids and the rest of the LGBTQ community can expose families to hatred and danger. One parent in Georgia told me that after she organized the first Pride celebration in her town, she received warrants for her arrest listing a dozen city and state violations, among them "enticing a child for indecent purposes." (The charges, which were traced back to a right-wing activist organization, were dismissed by a judge before being brought to trial.)

About the Author

Marla Broadfoot is a freelance science writer who lives in North Carolina. She has a Ph.D. in genetics and molecular biology and is an adjunct at the University of North Carolina at Chapel Hill. Her feature on a new type of pain pill was published in our September 2024 issue.

Evidence Undermines 'Rapid Onset Gender Dysphoria' Claims

By O. Rose Broderick

A recent study claiming to describe more than 1,600 possible cases of a "socially contagious syndrome" was retracted in June for failing to obtain ethics approval from an institutional review board. The survey examined "rapid-onset gender dysphoria," a proposed condition that attributes adolescent gender distress to exposure to transgender people through friends or social media. The existence of such a syndrome has been the subject of intense debate for the past several years and has fueled arguments against transgender rights reforms, despite being widely criticized by medical experts.

The American Psychological Association and 61 other health care providers' organizations signed a letter in 2021 denouncing the validity of rapid-onset gender dysphoria (ROGD) as a clinical diagnosis. And a steadily growing body of scientific evidence demonstrates that it does not reflect transgender adolescents' experiences and that "social contagion" is not causing more young people to seek gender-affirming care. Still, the concept continues to be used to justify anti-trans legislation across the U.S.

"To even say it's a hypothesis at this point, based on the paucity of research on this, I think is a real stretch," says Eli Coleman, former president of the World Professional Association for Transgender Health. Coleman helped create the organization's most recent standards of care for trans people, which endorse and explain the evidence for forms of gender-affirming care.

Many transgender people experience gender dysphoria, meaning that the gender that was assigned to them at birth and their gender identity don't align, causing distress. ROGD was proposed as a gender dysphoria subtype in a 2018 paper by physician and researcher Lisa Littman, then at Brown University.* Littman's survey asked parents of transgender adolescents—recruited predominantly from anti-transgender websites and forums–to describe their child's "sudden or rapid onset of gender dysphoria" and to state if it coincided with increased social media usage or the child's friends coming out as transgender.

Littman later issued a correction that updated the methodology, including a brief description of the websites and forums, and noted that ROGD is not a formal diagnosis. But the concept had already been taken upin books and podcasts–and by politicians–to promulgate the idea that peer pressure and social media are making kids transgender or that being transgender is a form of mental illness. As legislation targeting trans people has reached anall-time high in the U.S., ROGD's alleged social contagion has been invoked by lawmakers in states such as Missouri,Utah andArkansas to justify banning or restricting gender-affirming care for young people.

"This is just a fear-based concept that is not supported by studies," says Marci Bowers, president of the World Professional Association for Transgender Health. The term ROGD is being used to "scare people or to scare legislators into voting for some of these restrictive policies that take away options for young people. It's cruel, cruel legislation."

Like the 2018 study that coined the term rapid-onset gender dysphoria, the recently retracted paper, which was published this March in *Archives of Sexual Behavior*, surveyed parents of transgender children about their children's experiences. The study was co-authored by Michael Bailey, a psychologist at Northwestern University, and Suzanna Diaz, a pseudonym used by a mother of a child with gender dysphoria. Diaz is not affiliated with an institution and had already collected the survey data before collaborating with Bailey on the paper. The study was retracted because Diaz and Bailey did not get consent from the survey's respondents to have their responses published, although Bailey disputes this. (Bailey declined to answer questions about the retraction from *Scientific American*.)

The participants in both the 2018 and the retracted 2023 studies were recruited from online communities that were explicitly critical about many aspects of gender-affirming care for transgender kids. Littman's research was inspired in part by parents' posts on these skeptical websites.

In response to criticisms that recruiting parents from anti-transgender websites may have biased the results, Littman says, "I reject the premise that parents who believe transition will harm their children are more likely to discredit their kids' experiences than parents who believe that transition will help their children."

Most experts cite the survey of parents rather than transgender children themselves as another major flaw in the methodology of both studies.

Diane Ehrensaft, director of mental health at the University of California, San Francisco, Child and Adolescent Gender Center, concurs. "To talk about what children are thinking, feeling and doing, particularly as they get old enough to have their own minds and narratives, you need to interview them," she says.

Parents can often be the last to know about their child's gender identity, Ehrensaft says. Coming out can be terrifying for many transgender kids. Family members often respond with violence or distrust or may even kick the child out of the house. Almost 40 percent of transgender youth experience homelessness or housing instability, according to a 2022 report from the Trevor Project, a nonprofit that provides crisis support for young LGBTQ+ people. Many kids who wait to discuss their gender identity with their parents before appearing to "suddenly" come out are simply keeping themselves safe, Ehrensaft says.

"It is not rapid-onset gender dysphoria," she says. "It's rapid-onset parental discovery."

Many experts have also questioned what length of time qualifies as a "sudden" experience of gender dysphoria. Both the 2018 and 2023 studies left the definition up for parental interpretation. Complicating this, there isn't one pathway or time line for being transgender, says Tey Meadow, a Columbia University sociologist who studies sexuality and gender. "For some people, it can evolve slowly. For others, it can evolve quickly," she says.

For most transgender youth seeking gender-affirming care, considerable time elapses between when they realize they may be transgender and when they receive such care. A recent analysis of 10 Canadian medical centers in the *Journal of Pediatrics* found that 98.3 percent of young people seeking gender-affirming care had realized more than a year prior that they may have been transgender. "If ROGD were a real thing, we would expect to see two discernible streams of patients coming in [to receive care]," says Greta Bauer, a co-author of the study and director of the Eli Coleman Institute for Sexual and Gender Health at the University of Minnesota Medical School. There would be a distinct group of adolescents with more recent knowledge about their gender identity going to clinics and another group that had had such knowledge for years. "But we didn't see that," she says.

Thomas Steensma, a psychologist at Amsterdam University Medical Centers who provides gender-affirming therapy, says he has not seen evidence of the "social contagion" component of ROGD, and he cautions against even using these terms. "Rapid means out of control, and contagion signals a warning, and that warning induces fear," he says. "There's no evidence that certain developmental pathways are more problematic or less beneficial or helpful than others" for a child's gender identity.

Steensma reports that he sees two "peaks" of referrals in his clinic: young adolescents and 15-year-olds. In a2020 study Steensma and his colleagues looked at adolescent referrals from 2000 to 2016 and found no measurable difference in the psychological functioning or the intensity of the gender dysphoria between more recent referrals and those who came to the clinic starting in 2000. If adolescents are presenting with a different form of gender dysphoria, Steensma has not seen it.

The researchers did observe a change in their referral population in recent years, however. More kids assigned female at birth have been transitioning in recent years than those assigned male at birth. Many studies have captured this difference–including the 2018 survey proposing ROGD–but experts are unsure of its cause.

Littman suggests that female-assigned kids are more susceptible to the "social contagion" of gender dysphoria because they feel social pressure more acutely than male-assigned kids. But Ehrensaft says nothing in the clinical literature corroborates this assertion. Instead she attributes this discrepancy to shifting cultural factors that influence how children express themselves and explore their identity. In our culture, Ehrensaft says, "there's a lot more gender stress for the boy in the tutu than the girl in the football uniform."

Other forms of gender incongruence, such as identifying as nonbinary or gender nonconforming, further challenge the idea that children should be forced to abide by traditional gender categories. And the best way to understand what kids are experiencing is to ask them questions and listen to their answers, Ehrensaft says.

"In some ways, [kids] are far more advanced than I am, as somebody in my 70s, about how they live and understand gender," Ehrensaft adds. "So if we want to really understand gender, turn to the experts–and that would be the youth themselves."

About the Author

O. Rose Broderick is a freelance science journalist and former news intern at Scientific American *whose work focuses on energy, disability and disaster. Follow Broderick on Bluesky.*

Courts Are Rejecting Politicized Attacks on Care for Trans Kids

By Dan Vergano

Ads attacking transgender people may have driven votes in the 2024 election, but bans on health care for trans teens are increasingly falling short, both in the courts and in medical reviews. Voices of reason can fight back, it turns out, against a manufactured moral panic.

Around 1.3 percent of middle school students in the U.S., children on the cusp of adolescence, identify as transgender. Acceptance and awareness of transgender individuals has grown, akin to a "Gender Revolution" as National Geographic called it in 2017. The acceptance, in part, triggered politicized attacks, some frankly weird, centered on banning trans people from sports and ending gender-affirming care for them.

Those attacks on trans kids might be effective politics, but they are lousy medicine. Courts and medical reviews are increasingly coming down on the side of gender-affirming care.

Put simply, gender-affirming care supports people's own views of themselves. If they want changes in pronouns, names, hairstyles, or clothing, puberty blocking treatment as adolescents, or hormone replacement therapy–that's okay. What matters is they receive comprehensive medical and psychological care along the way, whatever they and their parents decide. In the U.S. this approach is endorsed by the World Professional Association for Transgender Health and the Endocrine Society as well as a host of other medical organizations. "Critics of our gender-affirming care policy mischaracterize it as pushing medical or surgical treatments on youth; in fact, the policy calls for the opposite," wrote the then-president of the American Academy of Pediatrics, Moira Szilagyi, in 2022.

Nevertheless, since 2021, 27 states have erected laws or policies limiting minors' access to this care. These bans are "exacerbating the already high rates of depression, anxiety, and suicide attempts among this vulnerable population," according to the American Psychological Association. Tennessee's ban is now under review by the U.S. Supreme Court in *U.S. v. Skrmetti*, with nationwide implications.

In the meantime an Ohio appeals court in March blocked that state's ban on gender-affirming care for minors, saying it violated the state's constitution. That court also weighed in on medical standards in its decision: "The medical evidence and clinical experience presented in this case demonstrate that, when provided in appropriate circumstances, gender-affirming care can meaningfully improve the health and well-being of transgender adolescents," found the judges, noting lower rates of depression and other mental health issues. State medical experts testifying in favor of the ban had cited the usual criticisms of "sufficiency and quality of the research" and European restrictions (but not bans) of gender-affirming care for minors. But the judges didn't buy that, finding "the state did not present, and the trial court did not find, any contrary **evidence-based standards** [emphasis theirs] accepted by any nationally or internationally recognized professional medical groups," in the decision.

Fans of trans-care bans regularly employ arguments about insufficient evidence and European restrictions, spreading disinformation. In 2023, for example, Arkansas attorney general Tim Griffin responded to a federal judge blocking his state's ban, saying, "There is no scientific evidence that any child will benefit from these procedures," on X. This echoed his state's ban, which decried "the lack of any long-term longitudinal studies" on puberty-blocking drugs. In other words, we should wait a few decades, while kids suffer, to see if lifesaving care sufficiently satisfies lawmakers like the ones who believe trans kids are "demons" and "mutants." This moving-the-goalposts demand for extra evidence for gender-affirming care—embedded in Arkansas' original 2021 ban—has subsequently been copy-pasted into other state laws pushed by partisan religious activists. "These bans were produced as part of an intentional strategy by social and religious conservatives to demonize and scapegoat transgender people," said Indiana University constitutional law expert Steve Sanders, speaking last year at a Federalist Society event reported by *USA Today*.

Of course in reality plenty of evidence demonstrates gender-affirming care's benefits, as an Association of the Scientific Medical Societies in Germany review concluded in March. The German review also found "no proven effect treatment alternative," according to news reports. That joins a French medical review released in December, which also backed gender-affirming care. So much for European resistance.

The now-apparent outlier in all this is the U.K.'s National Health Service (NHS) Cass Review of gender-affirming care released in April of 2024, which claimed, surprise, "remarkably weak evidence" for the benefits of gender-affirming medicine. It led to a ban there on puberty blockers—medications that delay puberty—calling for them only within a clinical trial. (This suggestion remains unimplemented; you simply cannot conduct an ethical blinded test of puberty blockers.)

Reviews of the Cass Review have found math errors, outsized demands for evidence, and unethical recommendations among its flaws. U.S. and Australian specialists found that "the (Cass) Review obscures key findings, misrepresents its own data, and is rife with misapplications of the scientific method." It also inexplicably excluded clinicians who work with trans kids. "The fact that so many have taken such an error-filled document at face value, using it to drive policy for vulnerable children, is very unfortunate," University of Wollongong epidemiologist Gideon Meyerowitz-Katz concluded last August, in an eight-part review.

Back in the courtroom, the Cass Review has also failed to persuade a federal judge, who cited its "unfounded medical opinion[s]," in March. He instead blocked a Trump administration executive order banning funding for hospitals that provided gender-affirming treatment to people under 19, calling it "essential care."

One notable U.S. judge impressed by the Cass Review, or its brand of arguments, is Supreme Court justice Samuel Alito, a partisan in judicial robes. He relied on it in December arguments to argue for Tennessee's ban, despite the review not being evidence in the case. Alito's endorsement only underlines the political roots of the case against gender-affirming care.

Even some Republicans can't stomach this assault on people's lives. "These are gut-wrenching decisions that should be made by parents and should be advised by teams of doctors," said Governor Mike DeWine of Ohio. He vetoed that state's ban in 2023, only to be overridden by his legislature. We'll see if that argument carries the day, as it should, over the politicians who so far have proven willing to trample on kids.

About the Author

Dan Vergano is senior editor, Washington, D.C., at Scientific American*. He has previously written for Grid News, BuzzFeed News,* National Geographic *and* USA Today*. He is chair of the New Horizons committee for the Council for the Advancement of Science Writing and a journalism award judge for both the American Association for the Advancement of Science and the U.S. National Academies of Sciences, Engineering, and Medicine.*

Gender-Affirming Health Care Should Be a Right, Not a Crime

By Kristina R. Olson

In late March, the Arkansas State House and Senate voted to prohibit health care workers in the state from providing gender-affirming health care to transgender and other gender-diverse young people. While the decision was vetoed by the governor on April 5, the state legislature overrode that veto the next day. Meanwhile the Alabama State Senate approved a law in March to make it a felony for doctors to provide gender-affirming health care to transgender youth. And a bill proposed in North Carolina would outlaw gender-affirmative care for people younger than 21. Several other U.S. states are pursuing similar legislation, hot on the heels of a related decision in the U.K. that initially required a court order for transgender youth under age 16 to access thiscare (though that ruling has been partially reversed).

These laws are out of sync with the recommendations of the American Medical Association, the Endocrine Society, the Pediatric Endocrine Society, the American Academy of Pediatrics, the American Psychiatric Association and the American Academy of Child and Adolescent Psychiatry, who all agree that gender-affirmative treatments are an important option for transgender youth.

I'm a researcher who has been studying and working with transgender youth and their families for most of the past decade. As such, I often end up seated next to curious people with questions about trans youth at dinner parties or on planes. This is how I've discovered just how much misunderstanding and misinformation there is on this topic.

I often hear concern and criticism about the early ages at which people mistakenly believe young people are accessing irreversible surgeries and hormones. As outlined in guidelines from the

Endocrine Society, no medical interventions occur before the onset of puberty. After that time, *blockers*—or, more technically, gonadotropin-releasing hormone (GnRH) agonists—are the first option available to young people. Importantly, some will not want or seek puberty blockers. For those who do, and who gain access to them, the impact of blockers is reversible.

As University of California, San Francisco, pediatric endocrinologist Stephen Rosenthal explained to me, four decades ago researchers thought puberty blockers would be helpful in treating infertility. In studies, though, investigators quickly realized that blockers did the opposite: they reduced or eliminated the possibility of conception, though that effect was entirely reversible. This discovery suggested they might instead be used to treat a range of other health conditions impacted by sex hormones, such as breast and prostate cancer and endometriosis.

In 1981 studies reporting the use of blockers in children appeared in the medical literature, but their use was unrelated to transgender health care. The children first accessing blockers had a condition called central precocious puberty, which, as the name implies, means they began puberty early—as early as preschool years. Doctors found they could put these young children on blockers, and the progression of their puberty would stop. They also observed that the blockers were reversible—meaning when a child stopped receiving blockers, their puberty began where it had left off. This earned blockers another nickname: some came to refer to them as a pubertal "pause button."

Blockers would have been in common use for children with central precocious puberty when a 13-year-old transgender boy referred to as "B" was seen by health care professionals in the Netherlands in the late 1980s. As described in a 1998 case study, B had "wished to be a boy from early on." Throughout childhood, while excelling in school, he struggled emotionally and was in and out of therapy. At age 12, the study authors wrote, B's mom found a suicide note explaining "that [he] did not want to live any longer if [he] would enter puberty." B was in increasing distress.

This was the point at which B's medical team offered him the option of trying puberty blockers temporarily. These blockers would stop B's body from moving through the pubertal process that would further feminize it–as they had for children with precocious puberty at much young ages–and would give him time to "explore gender issues for an extended period, without being pressured by any physical developments," as the study put it.

B's case became part of the scientific record when he cameto a clinic for gender-affirming hormone treatment at age 16. The clinic's team had long provided hormonal care to adults and older teens who were transgender and quickly realized that with blockers came the prospect that some of the physical changes that some transgender adults had found most distressing when they were teens could be avoided. Further, if a child later opted out of blockers, puberty would continue.

These days, most young people who are transgender and who start blockers, like B, decide to later use gender-affirming hormones, though others start blockers and then stop or opt out of hormones. Most who choose to use blockers show no regrets. Twenty-two years after he started on blockers, the medical team following B, at that point a 35-year-old medical student, indicated that he "would do it all over again. B was happy with his life." A larger study of 70 transgender young people at the same Amsterdam clinic found improvements in overall mental health, depression and general functioning after the use of blockers. Several papers by other teams around the world have seen similar results, though other studies have not found significant changes or have had sample sizes that were too small for alterations to be detected.

Most researchers and clinicians will agree that, as with all health concerns, we would like larger, more comprehensive studies. Such investigations can provide recommendations about how to further refine treatment for those who seek it, maximizing benefits and minimizing potential risks.

Importantly, as Jules Gill-Peterson of the University of Pittsburgh points out in her book *Histories of the Transgender Child*, "the vast majority of [trans youth] lack access to competent, responsible, and affordable care in whatever form they might ideally ask for it." These young trans people, including many individuals from lower-income backgrounds, people of color and homeless youth, lack the financial means, insurance or support of the adults around them—including medical staff—to receive the care they seek.

Therefore, even without laws specifically aimed at restricting access to transgender health care, barriers already exist for many trans youth. If lawmakers are interested in improving the health of young people, including transgender youth, as they often claim in these debates, a better use of their time might be to focus on improving access to high-quality medical health care for all rather than restricting it for some.

About the Author

Kristina R. Olson is a professor of psychology at Princeton University, where she directs the Human Diversity Lab and the Trans Youth Project.

Anti-Trans Laws Will Have a Chilling Effect on Medicine

By Ashley Andreou

Every year March 31 marks Transgender Day of Visibility, a day when we should be celebrating the accomplishments of people who are trans, honoring their resilience and advocating loudly for their rights. Yet the growing onslaught of anti-trans legislation targeting the health-care decisions that families make with their doctors threatens to cast a shadow over this day.

In 2021 I lost a family member to the mental trauma of transgender discrimination, so I speak from a place of watching someone I love suffer from lack of support. These recent and proposed laws, none of which are grounded in evidence-based medicine, will affect the mental and physical health of adults and children and the families who support them.

I am in medical school, and I plan to specialize in psychiatry with the hope of working with people who are transgender or nonbinary. Instead of making me feel empowered to serve, the intent behind these laws makes me fearful for my future patients. The directive in Texas that calls gender-affirming health care "child abuse" makes me afraid to practice and outraged that any state can insert itself into the clinical decision-making that we spend thousands of hours honing over several years. There are so few doctors who treat people who are transgender, let alone specialize in the physical and mental medicine specific to their needs. These laws could dissuade clinicians from entering this line of work.

Instead of enacting laws that deny the basic health rights of the trans community–and signal to trans individuals that they are not safe, accepted or supported–policy makers, clinicians and advocates need to work together to create laws that counteract and prevent the health disparities that are exacerbated by the enduring discrimination against this community.

One of the biggest points of misinformation in the lobbying for these laws is what constitutes gender-affirming health care. Gender-affirming care is defined as treatments that either delay the onset of physical changes associated with puberty or create physiological and physical changes that affirm one's gender identity (for example, hormone therapy or surgery). It is important to note that transitioning is a spectrum–not everyone who is transgender chooses hormone therapy, and not everyone chooses surgery. Yet all options are at stake with some of the laws that have passed or been proposed.

Doctors do not offer gender-affirming therapy rashly, and they prescribe puberty blockers only after working with a younger transgender person considering transition for a long time. Access to puberty blockers is critical because puberty's effects on certain body parts cannot be easily reversed by hormone therapy later in life (for example, testosterone's effects on voice). Altogether, the process requires coordinated counseling and medical oversight from a multidisciplinary clinical team that can include psychiatrists, endocrinologists and urologists, among others.

About 25 percent of transgender and nonbinary people choose gender-affirming surgery. Medical guidelines do not recommend surgery (such as facial reconstruction, mastectomy or phalloplasty) until a person is 18 years old, a point purposefully misrepresented by politicians who falsely say doctors are operating on young children.

More than 58,000 transgender teenagers who are transitioning are at risk of losing access to their medical care, according to a report from the University of California, Los Angeles, School of Law's Williams Institute. The effects of these bills and laws would be devastating. A large survey published in Pediatrics in 2018 found that 30 to 50 percent of young trans and nonbinary people reported a previous suicide attempt, compared with less than 9 percent of all adolescents.

Experts hypothesize that this greater suicide risk among trans youth is linked to internalized rejection and shame. In contrast, transgender youth who are supported by their families and receive gender-affirming care have markedly lower rates of depression: gender-affirming care has been associated with a nearly 40 percent reduction in depression and in attempting suicide in the past year. Furthermore, trans youth who have access to puberty suppressants have a much lower risk of lifetime suicide as adults.

As Texas's legislature debated anti-trans bills in 2021, the Trevor Project, an organization focused on LGBTQIA+ youth suicide prevention, received more than 10,800 total crisis contacts. Transgender or nonbinary youth made up more than 3,900 of those crisis contacts, and many of them reported feeling stressed, turning to self-harm and considering suicide as a result of the anti-LGBTQIA+ laws proposed by politicians in their state. Between 2020 and 2021, the Trevor Project recorded a 150 percent increase in LGBTQIA+ youth in Texas contacting the organization in crisis and seeking support. As a future psychiatrist, I find it incomprehensible that state lawmakers would willfully harm the mental health of so many young people.

All this legislation is at direct odds with the medical guidance of the American Psychiatric Association, the American Medical Association (AMA) and the American Academy of Pediatrics (AAP). These medical organizations recommend these medications and procedures for transgender individuals because there is a corpus of scientific literature affirming their benefits when medically indicated. These treatments are far from new and untested: puberty blockers have been used in medical care since the 1990s.

Calling me a child abuser will not stop my future patients from seeking care. Similar to the effects of efforts to stop abortion, transgender people and their families are liable to turn to unregulated black market products outside the purview of the Food and Drug Administration's monitoring of hormone product safety and quality. I can't fulfill the Hippocratic oath knowing that my inability to provide gender-affirming care might force patients into unsafe situations.

Numerous bills also propose criminalizing physicians if they offer transgender hormone therapy. In medical school, we had lectures on the importance of providing gender-affirming care, as well as panels specifically on the health-care experiences of transgender patients.

The closure in 2021 of Texas's only multidisciplinary clinic for transgender youth, GENECIS, in response to pressure from the governor is evidence of the stifling effect these laws have already had on medical professionals. [*Editor's Note: A court order allowed GENECIS to start taking patients again in May 2022, pending any appeals*.]

As highlighted by the pandemic, a dangerous risk factor for burnout among physicians is when they cannot control the health outcomes of their patients. Yet these bills go one step further, creating preventable negative health outcomes, and would introduce a new level of powerlessness and morale loss among providers. The AMA and AAP have both issued statements opposing recent anti-trans bills.

When speaking out against an anti-trans bill in Arkansas in 2021, Michele Hutchinson, a pediatrician at Arkansas Children's Hospital, said, "I guarantee you, if this bill passes, children will die. And I will call you guys every single time one does." In April 2021 that bill passed.

The day when police came to my house to tell my family that my uncle was found dead from an overdose after years of struggling with her identity, I felt like I was living through a nightmare.

In the painful days after, I committed myself to partnering with transgender communities to provide medical care and advocacy. Yet as legislators continue to signal that they would rather see people like my uncle dead than happy, alive and thriving, my grief has not subsided. Reading Texas Governor Greg Abbott's letter declaring gender-affirmative care "child abuse" and understanding that a growing number of legislators seek to bar me and other physicians from providing lifesaving care, I know my family's nightmare hasn't ended.

Despite these legal battles underscoring the transgender community's perseverance in the face of harrowing challenges, suffering is not what Transgender Day of Visibility is about.

Unfortunately, brazen and medically uninformed politicians denying basic human rights over binary ideas of gender have left us no choice but to rally and continue to fight. My uncle, who was a transgender woman but liked being called "uncle," deserved more in life. This is what I can do for her in death.

About the Author

Ashley Andreou is a psychiatry resident at New York-Presbyterian/Columbia University Irving Medical Center.

Why Anti-Trans Laws Are Anti-Science

By The Editors

On April 6, the Arkansas state legislature passed a law that would prohibit transgender youth from receiving gender-affirming medical care. It was not alone: before 2021 had even reached the halfway point, at least 35 similar bills—all of them in Republican-controlled states—had been proposed or passed, setting a regrettable record. Advocates for these laws argue that such treatments, which usually involve hormones that delay the changes associated with puberty, are unproven and dangerous and that the legislation is necessary to protect children. That is unscientific and cruel.

The actual danger comes from denying trans people the medical care they need. A 2020 study in the journal *Pediatrics* found that trans kids who wanted hormone treatments and did not receive them faced greater lifetime odds of suicidal thoughts than those who received "puberty blockers." These blockers, known as gonadotropin-releasing hormone analogues, are medically safe, and their effects are reversible. The medications have been in use for decades, most often in children who begin puberty too early. For trans kids, they buy some time for young people to explore their gender identity before their bodies develop permanent secondary sex characteristics such as breasts or Adam's apples. When they are ready, adolescents can decide whether to stop taking the blockers and continue to develop into the gender they were assigned at birth or to take gender-affirming hormones—testosterone or estrogen—to develop the features that match their gender identity.

Anti-trans laws play on fears that children may irreversibly alter their bodies and then come to regret it. But such scare tactics ignore reality for the vast majority of people who receive treatment. Under current guidelines from the Endocrine Society, none of these medical interventions can happen before the onset of puberty. Gender-affirming hormones are usually given in the teen years and only when patients have shown persistent, well-documented distress at the mismatch between their gender identity and their physical sex characteristics, according to the standards of care set by the World Professional Association for Transgender Health. And when it comes to the more significant step of genital surgery, the organization stipulates that it should be an option only for adults who have lived continuously for at least a year in the gender role congruent with their gender identity.

These laws would deny people safe treatments when getting them is already too hard. Many trans people—especially people of color, those from lower-income backgrounds and those who are homeless—do not have the financial resources or support they need to receive care. "If lawmakers are interested in improving the health of young people, including transgender youth, as they often claim in these debates, a better use of their time might be to focus on improving access to high-quality medical health care for all rather than restricting it for some," Kristina R. Olson, a Princeton University psychologist who studies the experiences of trans youth, wrote in a *Scientific American* opinion essay.

The statehouse war on trans people is not limited to bills restricting health-care access. At least 66 proposed laws would prohibit trans students from participating on sports teams consistent with their gender identity, and 15 would block trans people from using restrooms or locker rooms that match their gender identity, according to the Human Rights Campaign, an LGBTQ rights organization. These callous regulations are just the latest in a long barrage of Republican attacks on gay and trans people. The Trump White House rolled back many LGBTQ protections and even refused to acknowledge Pride Month, traditionally celebrated in June.

In contrast, President Joe Biden issued a presidential proclamation recognizing Pride Month and signed an executive order on his first day in office combating discrimination, on the federal level, on the basis of gender identity or sexual orientation. These and other acts by the Biden-Harris administration have increased desperately needed protections for the LGBTQ community, but they are just a start. Congress must pass the Equality Act, legislation that would establish nondiscrimination protections for LGBTQ people in employment, housing, credit, education, and other areas. The bill was passed by the House of Representatives in February but had not cleared the Senate at the time of this writing. And state lawmakers would do better to address the many real issues that hurt their constituents rather than enacting laws to combat nonexistent dangers.

Politics, Not Biology, Is Driving Legal Efforts to Classify Sex

By Agustín Fuentes

Amid the legal theater in the U.S. over sex and gender identity—triggered by a Trump administration decree that "'sex' shall refer to an individual's immutable biological classification as either male or female"—a moment of clarity has come from a judge.

In an ongoing military service case, federal district judge Ana Reyes stopped Jason Lynch, the Department of Justice attorney who has been defending the executive order, to ask, "You understand, as a matter of biology, it's just incorrect that there are only two sexes, right?" To which he responded, "I don't understand that to be incorrect." The judge then enlightened Lynch about the existence of intersex human beings, about whom he had confessed to have no knowledge. That's despite the fact that Lynch has been representing the U.S. government on an "immutable biological classification" in a federal courtroom.

Another clear example comes in the February announcement by the Department of Health and Human Services that expands on the recent executive order's "sex-based definitions." This announcement informs federal agencies that, for the purposes of carrying out their duties, a "male" is anyone who has a reproductive system that produces sperm, and a "female" is anyone with one that produces eggs.

The courtroom exchange and the HHS edict highlight why and how too much of the current discussion and legal arguments about sex are about ideology and not biology.

The "why" here is that most folks, apparently including ones at the HHS, are unfamiliar with how sex categories are understood by biologists and what the actual range of biological variation is in humans. This lack of familiarity enables idealogues to deploy distortions to achieve their agendas of exclusion. The decrees are barbs in culture wars, over gender issues and the rights of transgender people, as the *New York Times* has noted. The "how" is in the intentional assertions about sex categories and the human experience that are biologically inaccurate.

Clear definitions of categories matter in the law. The use of two sex categories to talk about a species is standard in biology. In many animal species, including people, however, there are individuals who are neither male nor female or who are sometimes both. In other species, there are two sexes, but they aren't male and female (usually these are intersex and male). And a few species have only one sex (usually female). The biological reality is that "male" and "female" are not universal immutable biological classifications but rather descriptions of typical patterns in reproductive biology. These categories, male and female, are used by biologists who fully understand that they rarely represent all the relevant biological variation in any given species or identical sets of variation across different species.

Sex is not one single, simple, uniform biological reality. Thus, biology cannot be invoked as a basis for such in legal terms. That's the bottom line.

Of course, men and women are not the same, and reproductive biology does structure important aspects of human bodies and lives. But none of the key biological systems associated with sex in humans (chromosomes, gonads, genetics, hormones, and so on) come exclusively in two "immutable" categories. Yes, most humans have either XX or XY chromosomes, but as Judge Reyes noted, some don't. People with either testes or ovaries are most common, but some people have both, and a few have ovotestes. Usually those with testes can produce sperm, and those with ovaries produce ova–but not always. The chromosomes one has do not always predict one's gonads or one's genitals or even all the elements of one's reproductive tract. It is true that most people have the "typical" combo of chromosomes, gonad and genitals, yet there are tens of millions of people alive right now who don't. These people are not errors, aberrations or problems; they are a part of the range of variation in our species. They are all real people. In fact, many who have these variations don't even know it. You might be one of them.

In making laws, then, we need to recognize what the actual range of variation in sex-related biology is and how it maps across everyone.

Consider height: Male individuals are, on average, about 8 percent taller than female ones. But most people are not average. If you drew a random set of 50 individuals (25 male and 25 female) and lined them up by height, the result would not be all the people who were male on one side and all those who were female on the other. Rather there would (usually) be a majority of male individuals in the taller half and a majority of female individuals in the shorter half. Averages aside, not *every* male person is larger than *every* female person. It's not just height either. In a recent National Health and Nutrition Examination Survey dataset, in the fifth to 95th weight percentiles, nonpregnant females aged 20 and older weighed between 110 and 263 pounds, and males in the same age range weighed between 136 and 287 pounds. As such, much of the variation—that space between 136 and 263 pounds—is an overlapping mix of female and male adults. This overlap and frequent lack of clear sex distinction extends beyond height and weight to livers, brains, hearts, stomachs, intestines, bones, etcetera.

Yes, there are some typical bodily differences between female and male adults of the same height and weight, such as upper-body muscle density and some specific hormone levels (but not kinds of hormones). How those differences manifest, how they developed, and what they mean for any given experience or ability, however, are not anywhere near an "immutable biological classification." The distribution of human biological variation, as it relates to one's capacity to serve in the military, sports abilities, childcare capacities, interest in math, love of cooking and everything else, is not simply, cleanly or "immutably" divided between the categories of female and male.

This administration's definitions of "sex" are intentionally designed to mislead the public about human biology. Any biologist knows this, and Judge Reyes pointed it out as an issue of legal concern. From a legal perspective, I guess those in the administration have the right to make any statement they wish as a reflection of their political ideology. But they do not have the right to invoke biology as a "natural" proof of their position–because it is not. There are few easy or universal biological "rules" dividing sex categories and human lives, but there are important variation and patterns. Biologists and other scientists need to help judges and attorneys understand what biology does and does not tell us about human sex and reject arguments that intentionally mispresent these data.

Falsehoods should not be enshrined in our laws. People's lives depend on it.

About the Author

Agustín Fuentes is a professor of anthropology at Princeton University. He is the author of Why We Believe: Evolution and the Human Way of Being *and* Race, Monogamy *and* Other Lies They Told You: Busting Myths about Human Nature.

The U.K.'s Cass Review Badly Fails Trans Children

By Cal Horton & Ruth Pearce

In the past decade, an escalating moral panic over transgender people's existence has embroiled both the U.K. and the U.S. Fear over the experience of children in particular has been stoked by years of provocative media coverage and political posturing. Common disinformation includes baseless claims that trans children are the victims of a "psychic epidemic" or "social contagion," that they're being "transitioned" against their will or that they are rushed through medical procedures.

Amid campaigns to roll back legal protections and health care provision for trans people in 2020, the U.K.'s National Health Service (NHS) launched the Cass Review of publicly funded gender services for children in England. Led by retired pediatrician Hilary Cass, the review examined existing research on trans health care interventions for people under age 18, consulted with stakeholders and made recommendations for NHS England services.

The final Cass Review report was released in April. It expresses concern about the number of young trans people presenting at doctors' offices for treatment and argues there is "remarkably weak evidence" for the benefits of gender-affirming medical interventions. It recommends, for instance, that puberty blockers–medications given to delay puberty–be provided only within a clinical trial. For younger children not yet facing puberty, it raises warnings about social transition–that is, nonmedical decisions kids may make for themselves such as changing their name, wearing different clothes or choosing to be referred to by a different pronoun.

While the Cass Review has been presented by the U.K. media, politicians and some prominent doctors as a triumph of objective inquiry, its most controversial recommendations are based on prejudice rather than evidence. Instead of helping young people, the review has caused enormous harm to children and their families, to democratic discourse and to wider principles of scientific endeavour. There is an urgent need to critically examine the actual context and findings of the report.

Since its 2020 inception, the Cass Review's anti-trans credentials have been clear. It explicitly excluded trans people from key roles in research, analysis and oversight of the project, while sidelining most practitioners with experience in trans health care. The project centered and sympathized with anti-trans voices, including professionals who deny the very existence of trans children. Former U.K. minister for women and equalities Kemi Badenoch, who has a history of hostility toward trans people even though her role was to promote equality within the government, boasted that the Cass Review was only possible because of her active involvement.

The methodology underpinning the Cass Review has been extensively criticized by medical experts and academics from a range of disciplines. Criticism has focused especially on the effect of bias on the Cass approach, double standards in the interpretation of data, substandard scientific rigor, methodological flaws and a failure to properly substantiate claims. For example, although the existing literature reports a wide range of important benefits of social transition and no credible evidence of harm, the Cass Review cautions against it. The review also dismisses substantial documented benefits of adolescent medical transition as underevidenced while highlighting risks based on evidence of significantly worse quality. A warning about impaired brain maturation, for instance, cites a single, very short speculative paper that in turn rests on one experimental study with female mice. Meanwhile extensive qualitative data and clinical consensus are almost entirely ignored. These issues help explain why the Cass recommendations differ from previous academic reviews and expert guidance from major medical organisations such as the World Professional Association for Transgender Health (WPATH) and the American Academy of Pediatrics.

WPATH's experts themselves highlight the Cass report's "selective and inconsistent use of evidence," with recommendations that "often do not follow from the data presented in the systematic reviews." Leading specialists in transgender medical care from the U.S. and Australia emphasize that "the Review obscures key findings, misrepresents its own data, and is rife with misapplications of the scientific method." For instance, the Cass report warns that an "exponential change in referrals" to England's child and adolescent gender clinic during the 2010s is "very much faster than would be expected." But this increase has not been exponential, and the maximum 5,000 referrals it notes in 2021 represents a very small proportion of the 44,000 trans adolescents in the U.K. estimated from 2021 census data.

The Cass report received rapturous support from all sectors of the U.K. media and swift endorsement from the two biggest U.K. political parties, the Conservatives and Labour. It was celebrated as proof that trans rights had indeed "gone too far," validating years of hateful propaganda. Many politicians and commentators eschewed any mention of the dangers and harms built into Cass's recommendations. These harms are already being acutely felt by trans children and adolescents around the U.K. and beyond. The Endocrine Society warned that "misinformation about gender-affirming care is being politicized."

Young trans people across the U.K. now face a plethora of abuses and humiliations promoted and legitimized by the Cass Review. Families, schools and social services have been cautioned against supporting social transition, advice that will keep trans children in situations of prolonged rejection and shame. Newly established gender services in England are not allowed to offer affirming care, instead focusing on invasive and exhaustive assessment. Being trans is regarded as an inherent problem, not a legitimate human identity.

There is currently no pathway to begin NHS medical transition for those under age 18 in the U.K. Puberty blockers are available only hypothetically, through a proposed clinical trial that has not even been designed, much less launched. Whether this unethical trial actually happens is beside the point–it is a tool for the NHS and the U.K. government to deflect accusations of a ban on adolescent health care.

In May the outgoing Conservative government exercised rarely used emergency powers to criminalize possession of puberty blockers sourced privately from outside the NHS. Following the Labour party's victory in the subsequent general election, new health minister Wes Streeting stated his support for the ban, citing the Cass Review. Criminalization only applies to trans youth: cisgender children and adolescents can still legally access puberty blockers for the same purpose–pausing puberty–and the same medicines continue to be prescribed for a broad range of other conditions and uses.

We estimate more than 1,000 trans adolescents in the U.K. now find that their treatment is illegal. Families risk an up to two-year prison sentence for supporting a child's continued access to private medication. These adolescents face a state-mandated medical detransition, forcing them to go through a puberty they have fought hard to avoid. The alternative is to flee the country or take greater risks: continue blockers under threat of prosecution or receive alternative medication with more frequent and severe side effects. Families are telling us that fear is driving trans children to discontinue routine hormone monitoring checks and to disengage with wider health care services.

Trans young people have for many years been under severe stress in the U.K. and worldwide, facing growing hostility, persecution and violence. Trans communities and supportive families are now desperately seeking to highlight current threats to young trans people's safety. In July a group of trans teenagers staged a dramatic four-day sit-in at NHS England headquarters, protesting under the slogan "trans kids deserve better." The systemic power imbalance that leaves trans youth vulnerable in the U.K. was yet again demonstrated when the U.K. media mostly ignored this unprecedented action.

Trans children now need louder allies from across the wider public, as well as the academic, medical and political establishments.

We must clearly call out the gross failures of the Cass Review, acknowledge the violent harms it has already enabled and work proactively to defend all children's access to prejudice-free health care.

Cal Horton is a research fellow in applied trans studies at Oxford Brookes University's Center for Diversity, Policy, Research and Practice in England.

About the Author

Ruth Pearce is a lecturer in community development at the Glasgow University School of Education in Scotland and senior fellow at the Center for Applied Transgender Studies in Chicago. She is author of the book Understanding Trans Health and editor of the Community Development Journal.

How Medicine's Fixation on the Sex Binary Harms Intersex People

By Meghan McDonough

In the summer of 1996 a small group of people met in northern California to share their experiences with intersex variations. One participant, Heidi Walcutt, said that doctors surgically reduced her clitoris as a young child "to more closely approximate a normal female appearance."

This resulted in nerve damage that would blunt sexual sensation later in life, as well as stigma that made Walcutt feel at times like hiding in the closet and at other times intensely angry. Others in the group similarly reported shame, confusion and anger resulting from their medical treatment.

The encounter was archived in a documentary created by the Intersex Society of North America, which was founded just three years earlier by an activist using the name Cheryl Chase, whose experience paralleled that of Walcutt. (Chase's name is now Bo Laurent.)

Intersex is an umbrella term for variations in reproductive or sexual anatomy that may appear in a person's chromosomes, genitals or internal organs, and it has been estimated to include about 1.7 percent of the population. There are more than 30 medical terms for different combinations of sex traits that fall outside of the typical "male" and "female" paths of development.

In the second episode of *Scientific American*'s documentary series A Question of Sex, we look at how people with sex variations are challenging longstanding notions of the sex binary in medicine.

In a survey conducted in 2020 by the Center for American Progress, nine in 10 LGBTQ+ intersex individuals reported some level of poor physical health. Of the majority who reported experiencing discrimination in the year prior, more than four in five said it had affected their financial well-being.

While international human rights groups widely condemn medically unnecessary intersex surgeries on minors, science has been slow to follow.

Genital surgeries on intersex youth first became commonplace in the 1950s, when a psychologist at Johns Hopkins University argued that a baby with genitals that looked neither clearly male nor female should be assigned a sex in early age and that their body should be altered to match. If a penis or a clitoris was deemed too small or large, respectively, it was shaved down.

There are life-threatening conditions in which genital surgery is required for infants and children. But "normalizing" their genital appearance to match a sex assigned in early age isn't medically necessary and is still largely up to doctors and parents. Advocates have long argued that the decision should instead be delayed until individuals are old enough to give informed consent.

Sean Saifa Wall is an intersex activist and researcher who was born with an intersex variation called androgen insensitivity syndrome, which occurs when a person who has XY chromosomes is resistant to hormones called androgens.

At age 13, Wall underwent a surgery to remove his internal testes, which at the time were thought to carry a risk of cancer. He told *Scientific American* that, not long after, he and his mom attended a consultation with the same doctor for another cosmetic procedure that involved shaving down his clitoris and creating a cavity inside of him.

"There are so many assumptions made: that I would want a vagina, that I would want to be in a heterosexual relationship, that I would even identify as a woman."

Arlene Baratz is a physician who had to rethink what she was taught in medical school when she learned that her two daughters were born with intersex variations. She notes that the stigmatizing push to "treat" genital differences doesn't square with how science thinks about other traits that naturally vary in the population.

"I think we know through science that there is a spectrum of variation for just about everything, including sex traits," Baratz says. "And people with intersex bodies show us that because their bodies exist on a spectrum of difference. I think the issue is that people want to think about gender as a binary."

As a result, she explains, most research on surgery focuses on cosmetic outcomes. "They'll report that they're able to put something in the vagina that they create," Baratz says. "And being able to put something in there of a certain size, they say the surgery was a success but then no information about, when that person goes on to want to be a sexual person, how that's working out for them."

One of Baratz's daughters is now a psychiatrist who focuses on the mental health of LGBTQI people. In 2020 the two co-authored a study reflecting the need for more community-based research on the mental health of intersex people.

In July 2020, after years of activism by Wall, Baratz and others, Ann & Robert H. Lurie Children's Hospital of Chicago became the first in the country to say it would stop performing medically unnecessary surgeries on intersex infants and children.

Hospitals in other cities have since followed suit. And in 2021 New York City passed a bill to educate doctors, parents and guardians of intersex children on the potential harms of genital surgery.

After all, the fixation on a sex binary in science, Wall points out, doesn't occur in a vacuum.

"I think for people asking the question 'Is your child a boy or a girl?' I would really challenge them to just take a moment and ask, 'Why? Why is it so important?' Are you just happy to have a baby? Are you just happy to start a family? I think those are quality-of-life questions that often get overlooked or missed in this conversation."

About the Author

Meghan McDonough is a filmmaker and journalist based in Brooklyn, N.Y.

Supreme Court to Decide Landmark Transgender Health Care Case. Here's What's at Stake

By Allison Parshall

This week the U.S. Supreme Court heard oral arguments in *United States v. Skrmetti*, a case that challenges Tennessee's ban on gender-affirming care for minors. The justices are considering whether these bans discriminate on the basis of sex under the Constitution's Equal Protection Clause.

The Court appears poised to uphold the Tennessee law, SB1, which was enacted in July 2023 and prohibits all medical care intended to allow someone under 18 years old to "identify with, or live as, a purported identity inconsistent with the minor's sex" assigned at birth, citing the state's interest in "encouraging minors to appreciate their sex."

"What's at stake is whether the Court is going to consider transgender people to merit some of the protections of the Equal Protection Clause or whether states are allowed to discriminate against transgender people. And that's a big question," says Elana Redfield, an LGBTQ+ policy expert at the Williams Institute, part of the University of California, Los Angeles.

The Tennessee law, which mirrors similar recent bans in 24 other states, prevents transgender youth from receiving treatments proven to relieve the symptoms of gender dysphoria (psychological distress that results from an incongruence between someone's sex assigned at birth and their gender identity). These treatments include puberty-blocking drugs and hormone therapies–medications also used by nontransgender adolescents and children to treat a variety of conditions. Their use to treat gender dysphoria is supported by the American Medical Association, the American Association of Pediatrics, the American Psychological Association and other important medical institutions.

A number of studies have shown that adolescents who receive gender-affirming care have better mental health outcomes–including a lower rate of suicidal ideation–than those who wanted treatment but couldn't get it. And care bans have increased suicide rates among transgender young people in affected states, recent research has shown. Like any medication, the treatments can have risks, which is true when they are prescribed for nontransgender people as well. Parents and physicians weigh these risks against those of not receiving the care. Critics of gender-affirming care for minors often cite concerns that adolescents will later regret the treatment, but regret rates are relatively low.

While the Tennessee law prohibits these treatments when they are used for the purpose of transitioning, nontransgender youth continue to have access to them. In Supreme Court oral arguments on Wednesday U.S. Solicitor General Elizabeth Prelogar argued that this constitutes sex discrimination–because the law uses birth-assigned sex to determine what medications someone legally has access to. For example, an adolescent would be able to access testosterone if they were assigned male at birth but not if they were assigned female.

"SB1 leaves the same medications and many others entirely unrestricted when used for any other purpose [outside of gender-affirming care], even when those uses present similar risks," Prelogar said during her opening statement. The federal government is arguing that the law's sex-based classification should trigger a heightened level of judicial scrutiny under the Equal Protection Clause of the 14th Amendment to the Constitution. If the Supreme Court agrees, it can send the case back to the lower courts. There Tennessee officials would have to demonstrate that the law serves an important government interest. At this stage, the lower courts could weigh the evidence supporting gender-affirming care in evaluating the impacts of a total ban.

Before the Court's nine justices, Tennessee Solicitor General Matthew Rice argued that the law does not discriminate on the basis of sex because it prevents both those assigned male and female at birth from transitioning. This reasoning could also be applied to laws that prevent or restrict adults from receiving gender-affirming care, such as Florida's SB 254. A decision is not expected until next spring, but at least five members of the Supreme Court's conservative supermajority are widely seen as likely to side with Tennessee.

"If the Court upholds this ban, it will potentially validate all the 24 states that have bans" on gender-affirming hormone therapy for minors, Redfield says.* The decision, she adds, may impact current and future legal challenges to other antitrans legislation—such as bans on adult gender-affirming care or bathroom and sports bans based on gender identity.

The stakes of these challenges will continue to grow as President-elect Donald Trump returns to the White House in January. This election cycle, Republicans spent an estimated $215 million in network TV advertisements attacking and denigrating transgender people, who make up less than 1 percent of the U.S. population.

"On Day One, I will sign an executive order instructing every federal agency to cease the promotion of sex or gender transition at any age," Trump said at an event hosted by the anti-LGBTQ+ group Moms for Liberty in June 2023. He has also said that he would revoke the federal funding of any hospital or health care provider that provides gender-affirming care to minors.

This possibility is very worrying for Daphna Stroumsa, an ob-gyn at University of Michigan Health, who specializes in gender-affirming care. Being prevented from providing patients with the best care is "heartbreaking. It feels ethically and morally wrong," Stroumsa says. "The effects of not being able to offer this care on the individual can be devastating."

Susan Lacy, one of the plaintiffs in the case against Tennessee's ban and an ob-gyn based in Memphis, expressed similar distress in a declaration in the initial lawsuit. "Being prohibited from treating my patients in accordance with existing evidence and clinical guidelines is an awful scenario that no medical provider should be forced to face," she wrote.

Nearly 40 percent of transgender young people between the ages of 13 and 17 now live in states where laws have banned gender-affirming care. Members of the three families that challenged Tennessee's ban in this case, which originated in a Tennessee district court, have described how devastating a prohibition would be for their life and livelihood. In all three families, the parents described how their children experienced debilitating mental and physical symptoms of gender dysphoria that caused them to withdraw from the world. One child began getting repeated urinary tract infections because she was uncomfortable using the bathroom at school, her parents said. Another, referred to as Ryan Roe, threw up almost every morning before school and stopped talking almost entirely.

"I was scared and didn't want to move too fast with medical treatment," Roe's mother wrote in a declaration. "But I also worried, that in my fear, I had moved too slowly for what my child needed. As I watched my son suffer and decline, I realized we couldn't wait anymore." The family consulted a doctor about gender-affirming care, and Roe eventually started taking testosterone. He subsequently "transformed back into the vocal, outgoing child that we saw before puberty," his mother said.

"Nobody makes this choice overnight," Stroumsa says. "These are dedicated parents and dedicated physicians who have a very long process ... before any decisions are made."

All three families are considering traveling out of state regularly for treatment–an expensive effort that requires parents to take days off of work and children to miss school. And clinics in states without bans already have limited capacity. "We're in the state of Michigan, which is within travel distance for multiple states with bans," Stroumsa says. "We've seen a rise in patients coming from out of state, and we're already booking several months out for consultations."

But for all three families, going back to the way things used to be is not an option.

"This might seem like a small issue to others but it affects my whole world," wrote John Doe, an adolescent transgender boy, in a declaration submitted to the district court. "I've gone through a lot to finally get to the happy, healthy place where I am and I desperately hope that doesn't all get taken away from me."

About the Author

Allison Parshall is associate editor for mind and brain at Scientific American *and she writes the weekly online Science Quizzes. As a multimedia journalist, she contributes to* Scientific American's *podcast* Science Quickly. *Parshall's work has also appeared in* Quanta Magazine *and Inverse. She graduated from New York University's Arthur L. Carter Journalism Institute with a master's degree in science, health and environmental reporting. She has a bachelor's degree in psychology from Georgetown University.*

GLOSSARY

ambiguity Being unclear or having more than one meaning.

androgenic Something possessing both male and female characteristics.

autonomy The ability to make your own decisions and act independently without control from others.

bioethicist A person who analyzes dilemmas that arise from medicine, biology, and technology and ensures ethical principles are followed.

bone density The amount of calcium and other minerals in bones, indicating its durability.

congruence Two or more objects in agreement.

cryptopreservation The use of extremely low temperatures to store biological cells.

emotional intelligence The ability to understand and manage your own emotions in a positive way.

endocrinologist A doctor who specializes in hormone imbalances and disorders.

hypergonadism A condition in which the sex glands in a person are overactive, which can lead to rapid physical changes.

incongruence Being inconsistent or incompatible.

marginalized Individuals or groups treated as inferior, insignificant, or outside the mainstream of society.

mastectomy The surgical removal of all breast tissue.

neuroscience The study of the nervous system, including the brain and nerves.

ostracization To exclude a person from a group or social circle on purpose.

pseudonym A fake name adopted by a person to hide their real identity.

resilience The ability to recover quickly from difficulties.

scrutinized To examine something very carefully.

stigma A strong feeling against a person, often based on stereotypes.

suppression Holding back something from happening.

FURTHER INFORMATION

Ainsworth, Claire, and Nature Magazine. "Sex Redefined: The Idea of 2 Sexes Is Overly Simplistic." *Scientific American*. October 22, 2018. www.scientificamerican.com/article/sex-redefined-the-idea-of-2-sexes-is-overly-simplistic1/.

Ashley, Florence, Shari Brightly-Brown, and G. Nic Rider. "Beyond the Trans/Cis Binary: Introducing New Terms will Enrich Gender Research." *Nature*. June 10, 2024. www.nature.com/articles/d41586-024-01719-9.

Haupt, Sue, Cheryl Carcel, and Robyn Norton. "Neglecting Sex and Gender in Research is a Public-Health Risk." *Nature*. May 15, 2024. www.nature.com/articles/d41586-024-01372-2.

Kennis, Mathilde, Robin Staicu, Marieke Dewitte, Guy T'Sjoen, Alexander T. Sack, and Felix Duecker. "Heed Lessons from Past Studies Involving Transgender People: First, do no Harm." *Nature*. May 28, 2024. www.nature.com/articles/d41586-024-01521-7.

Parshall, Allison. "Supreme Court Weighs Ban on Scientifically Discredited 'Conversion Therapy'." *Scientific American*. October 7, 2025. www.scientificamerican.com/article/supreme-court-weighs-colorados-ban-on-scientifically-discredited-conversion/.

Ritz, Stacey A., and Lorraine Greaves. "We Need More-Nuanced Approaches to Exploring Sex and Gender in Research." *Nature*. May 1, 2024. www.nature.com/articles/d41586-024-01204-3.

Roselli, C.E. "Neurology of Gender Identity and Sexual Orientation." National Library of Medicine. August 2, 2019. pmc.ncbi.nlm.nih.gov/articles/PMC6677266/.

Rosenthal, G. Samantha, and The Conversation US. "Pseudoscience Has Long Been Used to Oppress Transgender People." *Scientific American*. February 12,

2024. www.scientificamerican.com/article/pseudoscience-has-long-been-used-to-oppress-transgender-people/.

Russo, Francine. "Is There Something Unique about the Transgender Brain?" *Scientific American*. January 1, 2016. www.scientificamerican.com/article/is-there-something-unique-about-the-transgender-brain/.

CITATIONS

1.1 What the Science on Gender-Affirming Care for Transgender Kids Really Shows by Heather Boerner (May 12, 2022); 1.2 Transgender Youth Have Better Emotional Health after Taking Hormones, New Study Finds by Tyler Santora (February 25, 2025); 1.3 Transgender Kids: What Does It Take to Help Them Thrive? by Francine Russo (January 1, 2016); 1.4 What Are Puberty Blockers, and How Do They Work? by Allison Parshall (May 1, 2023); 2.1 When Real Life Is Hostile, LGBTQ+ Gamers Find Friendship Online by Shannon Liao (March 19, 2024); 2.2 The Disturbing History of Research into Transgender Identity by Jack Turban (October 23, 2020); 2.3 Sex and Gender Map onto Different Brain Networks in Children by Allison Parshall (July 12, 2024); 2.4 Is There Something Unique about the Transgender Brain? by Francine Russo (January 1, 2016); 2.5 There Are No Such Things as Gendered Emotions by Pragya Agarwal (June 24, 2024); 3.1 Sports Celebrate Physical Variation–Until It Challenges Social Norms by Bethany Brookshire (October 1, 2024) 3.2 Hormone Levels Are Being Used to Discriminate against Female Athletes by Grace Huckins (February 1, 2021); 3.3 The Long History of Sex Testing in the Olympics and Other Elite Sports by Rachel Feltman, Fonda Mwangi & Jeffery DelViscio (July 31, 2024); 4.1 How Junk Science Is Being Used against Trans Kids by Tulika Bose (April 8, 2022); 4.2 RFK, Jr., Releases Report Attacking Medical Care for Trans Children by Dan Vergano (November 19, 2025); 4.3 Laws Vilifying Transgender Children and Their Families Are Abusive by Tey Meadow & Kristina R. Olson (March 29, 2022); 4.4 How Anti-LGBTQ+ Rhetoric Fuels Violence by Helen Santoro (December 12, 2022); 4.5 Families Find Ways to Protect Their LGBTQ Kids by Marla Broadfoot (March 19, 2024); 4.6 Evidence Undermines 'Rapid Onset Gender Dysphoria' Claims by O. Rose Broderick (August 24, 2023); 4.7 Courts Are Rejecting Politicized Attacks on Care for Trans Kids by Dan Vergano (March 26, 2025); 4.8 Gender-Affirming Health Care Should Be a Right, Not a Crime by Kristina R. Olson (April 13, 2021); 4.9 Anti-Trans Laws Will Have a Chilling Effect on Medicine by Ashley Andreou (March 31, 2022); 4.10 Why Anti-Trans Laws Are Anti-Science by The Editors (June 30, 2021); 4.11 Politics, Not Biology, Is Driving Legal Efforts to Classify Sex by Agustín Fuentes (February 25, 2025) 4.12 The U.K.'s Cass Review Badly Fails Trans Children by Cal Horton & Ruth Pearce (August 7, 2024); 4.13 How Medicine's Fixation on the Sex Binary Harms Intersex People by Meghan McDonough (August 24, 2022); 4.14 Supreme Court to Decide Landmark Transgender Health Care Case. Here's What's at Stake by Allison Parshall (December 5, 2024).

INDEX